50 St. Patrick's Day Baking Recipes for Home

By: Kelly Johnson

Table of Contents

- Classic Irish Soda Bread
- Green Velvet Cupcakes
- Shamrock Sugar Cookies
- Guinness Chocolate Cake
- Leprechaun Pie
- Mint Chocolate Chip Cookies
- Irish Cream Cheesecake
- Pot o' Gold Cupcakes
- Green Macarons
- Lucky Charms Rice Krispies Treats
- St. Patrick's Day Brownies
- Irish Apple Cake
- Green Tea Muffins
- Irish Shortbread Cookies
- Lucky Leprechaun Brownies
- Green Velvet Whoopie Pies
- Mint Brownie Cheesecake Bars
- Irish Cream Brownies
- Shamrock-shaped Donuts
- Guinness Stout Cupcakes
- Green Pistachio Cake
- Lemon and Lime Bars
- Irish Buttercream Frosting
- St. Patrick's Day Cheesecake Swirl Brownies
- Green Jello Cupcakes
- Minty Chocolate Fondue
- Shamrock Cheesecake Bites
- Irish Potato Candy
- Green Cinnamon Rolls
- Irish Whiskey Cake
- Matcha Cupcakes
- Lucky Clover Cake Pops
- Shamrock Cream Puffs
- Green Tea and White Chocolate Cookies
- St. Patrick's Day Tiramisu
- Chocolate Mint Poke Cake

- Irish Soda Bread Muffins
- Green Coconut Macaroons
- Guinness and Chocolate Cupcakes
- Shamrock Cake Roll
- Irish Brown Bread Muffins
- Mint Chocolate Chip Cheesecake
- Lucky Charms Marshmallow Treats
- St. Patrick's Day Mini Bundt Cakes
- Green Sugar Cookie Bars
- Irish Cream Fudge
- Shamrock Pie
- Green Velvet Cake Pops
- Mint Oreo Cheesecake Bars
- Leprechaun Cupcake Jars

Classic Irish Soda Bread

Ingredients:

- 4 cups all-purpose flour
- 1 teaspoon baking soda
- 1/2 teaspoon salt
- 1 3/4 cups buttermilk
- 1/4 cup granulated sugar (optional, for a touch of sweetness)
- 1 cup raisins or currants (optional, for added texture and sweetness)

Instructions:

1. **Preheat the Oven:**
    - Preheat your oven to 425°F (220°C). Place a rack in the middle position.
2. **Prepare the Dry Ingredients:**
    - In a large bowl, whisk together the flour, baking soda, and salt. If using sugar, add it to the mixture.
3. **Add Raisins (if using):**
    - Gently fold in the raisins or currants, if desired.
4. **Mix Wet Ingredients:**
    - Make a well in the center of the dry ingredients. Pour in the buttermilk and mix gently with a wooden spoon or your hands until just combined. The dough will be sticky.
5. **Shape the Dough:**
    - Turn the dough out onto a floured surface. With floured hands, gently shape the dough into a round loaf. Place it on a lightly floured baking sheet or in a cast-iron skillet.
6. **Score the Dough:**
    - Using a sharp knife, cut a deep cross (about 1/4 inch) on top of the dough. This helps the bread cook evenly and gives it a traditional look.
7. **Bake the Bread:**
    - Bake in the preheated oven for about 35-45 minutes, or until the bread is golden brown and sounds hollow when tapped on the bottom.
8. **Cool:**
    - Remove the bread from the oven and let it cool on a wire rack.
9. **Serve:**
    - Slice and serve with butter, jam, or cheese. Enjoy your classic Irish soda bread warm or at room temperature.

Tips:

- **Buttermilk Substitute:** If you don't have buttermilk, you can make a quick substitute by adding 1 tablespoon of lemon juice or white vinegar to a measuring cup and filling it up with milk to make 1 3/4 cups. Let it sit for 5-10 minutes before using.

- **Add-Ins:** Feel free to add other mix-ins like caraway seeds or chopped nuts for extra flavor.

This bread is best enjoyed fresh but can be stored in an airtight container for a few days. It also makes excellent toast!

Green Velvet Cupcakes

Ingredients:

For the Cupcakes:

- 1 1/2 cups all-purpose flour
- 1 cup granulated sugar
- 1/2 teaspoon baking soda
- 1/2 teaspoon baking powder
- 1/2 teaspoon salt
- 1/2 cup vegetable oil
- 1 large egg
- 1/2 cup buttermilk
- 1 tablespoon green food coloring (gel or liquid)
- 1 tablespoon cocoa powder
- 1 teaspoon vanilla extract
- 1 teaspoon white vinegar

For the Cream Cheese Frosting:

- 1/2 cup unsalted butter, softened
- 8 oz cream cheese, softened
- 4 cups powdered sugar
- 1 teaspoon vanilla extract
- A pinch of salt

Instructions:

1. Preheat the Oven:

- Preheat your oven to 350°F (175°C). Line a 12-cup muffin tin with cupcake liners.

2. Prepare the Dry Ingredients:

- In a medium bowl, whisk together the flour, sugar, baking soda, baking powder, salt, and cocoa powder.

3. Mix the Wet Ingredients:

- In a large bowl, combine the oil, egg, buttermilk, food coloring, vanilla extract, and vinegar. Mix well.

4. Combine Ingredients:

- Gradually add the dry ingredients to the wet ingredients, mixing until just combined. Be careful not to overmix; a few lumps are okay.

5. Fill the Cupcake Liners:

- Divide the batter evenly among the 12 cupcake liners, filling each about 2/3 full.

6. Bake the Cupcakes:

- Bake for 18-22 minutes, or until a toothpick inserted into the center comes out clean.

7. Cool:

- Allow the cupcakes to cool in the tin for about 5 minutes, then transfer them to a wire rack to cool completely.

8. Prepare the Frosting:

- While the cupcakes are cooling, make the frosting. In a large bowl, beat the softened butter and cream cheese together until smooth and creamy. Gradually add the powdered sugar, beating on low speed until combined. Add the vanilla extract and a pinch of salt, and beat until the frosting is fluffy.

9. Frost the Cupcakes:

- Once the cupcakes are completely cool, frost them with the cream cheese frosting. You can use a piping bag for a decorative touch or simply spread the frosting with a knife.

10. Optional Decoration:

- For extra flair, you can garnish with sprinkles, edible glitter, or a small shamrock decoration.

Tips:

- **Food Coloring:** Use gel food coloring for a more vibrant color. If using liquid food coloring, you might need to use a bit more to achieve the desired green.
- **Storage:** Store frosted cupcakes in an airtight container in the refrigerator. They'll stay fresh for about 3-4 days.

Enjoy these festive and delicious Green Velvet Cupcakes!

Shamrock Sugar Cookies

Ingredients:

For the Cookies:

- 2 3/4 cups all-purpose flour
- 1 1/2 teaspoons baking powder
- 1/2 teaspoon salt
- 1 cup unsalted butter, softened
- 1 1/2 cups granulated sugar
- 1 large egg
- 1 teaspoon vanilla extract
- 1/4 teaspoon almond extract (optional, for added flavor)

For the Glaze or Royal Icing:

- 2 cups powdered sugar
- 2 tablespoons milk (for glaze)
- 1 tablespoon lemon juice (for glaze)
- **For Royal Icing:** (alternative to glaze)
    - 1 egg white or 2 tablespoons meringue powder
    - 2 cups powdered sugar
    - 1/2 teaspoon lemon juice or vinegar
    - Water, as needed

Instructions:

1. Preheat the Oven:

- Preheat your oven to 350°F (175°C). Line baking sheets with parchment paper or silicone baking mats.

2. Prepare the Dry Ingredients:

- In a medium bowl, whisk together the flour, baking powder, and salt. Set aside.

3. Cream the Butter and Sugar:

- In a large bowl, beat the softened butter and sugar together until light and fluffy, about 3-4 minutes.

4. Add Egg and Extracts:

- Beat in the egg, vanilla extract, and almond extract (if using) until well combined.

5. Mix in Dry Ingredients:

- Gradually add the flour mixture to the wet ingredients, mixing until just combined. The dough will be thick.

6. Roll Out the Dough:

- On a lightly floured surface, roll out the dough to about 1/4-inch thickness. Use a shamrock-shaped cookie cutter to cut out shapes.

7. Bake the Cookies:

- Place the cookie cutouts on the prepared baking sheets. Bake for 8-10 minutes, or until the edges are lightly golden.

8. Cool:

- Allow the cookies to cool on the baking sheets for a few minutes, then transfer them to wire racks to cool completely.

9. Decorate:

- **For the Glaze:**
    - In a small bowl, whisk together the powdered sugar, milk, and lemon juice until smooth. If the glaze is too thick, add a little more milk. If it's too thin, add more powdered sugar. Use a spoon or a piping bag to drizzle or spread the glaze over the cooled cookies. Let the glaze set before serving.
- **For Royal Icing:**
    - If using meringue powder: In a large bowl, beat the meringue powder with water until soft peaks form. Gradually add powdered sugar and lemon juice until the mixture is smooth and glossy. Divide the icing into bowls and tint with food coloring as desired. Pipe the icing onto the cookies using a piping bag or squeeze bottle. Let the royal icing dry completely before storing.

Tips:

- **Chill the Dough:** If the dough is too soft to roll out, chill it in the refrigerator for about 30 minutes.
- **Food Coloring:** If you want to color the glaze or royal icing, use gel food coloring for best results.
- **Storage:** Store the decorated cookies in an airtight container at room temperature for up to a week.

Enjoy making and sharing these festive Shamrock Sugar Cookies!

Guinness Chocolate Cake

Ingredients:

For the Cake:

- 1 cup Guinness stout (or other dark stout beer)
- 1 cup unsalted butter
- 3/4 cup unsweetened cocoa powder
- 2 cups granulated sugar
- 1 1/2 cups all-purpose flour
- 1 1/2 teaspoons baking powder
- 1 1/2 teaspoons baking soda
- 1/2 teaspoon salt
- 2 large eggs
- 2/3 cup sour cream
- 1 teaspoon vanilla extract

For the Cream Cheese Frosting:

- 8 oz cream cheese, softened
- 1/2 cup unsalted butter, softened
- 4 cups powdered sugar
- 1 teaspoon vanilla extract

Instructions:

1. Preheat the Oven:

- Preheat your oven to 350°F (175°C). Grease and flour your cake pans or line them with parchment paper.

2. Heat the Stout and Butter:

- In a medium saucepan over medium heat, combine the Guinness and butter. Heat until the butter is melted. Remove from heat and whisk in the cocoa powder until smooth. Let it cool slightly.

3. Mix the Dry Ingredients:

- In a large bowl, sift together the flour, sugar, baking powder, baking soda, and salt.

4. Combine Wet Ingredients:

- In a separate bowl, beat the eggs, sour cream, and vanilla extract until well combined.

5. Combine All Ingredients:

- Gradually add the cooled stout mixture to the dry ingredients, mixing until just combined. Then fold in the egg mixture until smooth. Be careful not to overmix.

6. Bake the Cake:

- Divide the batter evenly between the prepared cake pans. Bake for 30-35 minutes, or until a toothpick inserted into the center comes out clean. If using an 8x8 inch pan, bake for about 40-45 minutes.

7. Cool:

- Allow the cakes to cool in the pans for about 10 minutes, then transfer to a wire rack to cool completely before frosting.

8. Prepare the Frosting:

- In a large bowl, beat the cream cheese and butter together until smooth. Gradually add the powdered sugar, beating on low speed until combined. Add the vanilla extract and beat until fluffy.

9. Frost the Cake:

- Once the cakes are completely cool, spread the cream cheese frosting evenly over the top and sides. If you prefer a smoother finish, you can chill the frosted cake for about 30 minutes before serving.

Tips:

- **Beer Choice:** Use a good quality stout for the best flavor. Guinness is a popular choice, but any dark stout will work.
- **Cake Storage:** Store the frosted cake in an airtight container in the refrigerator for up to 5 days. Bring to room temperature before serving for the best flavor.
- **Decorations:** You can decorate the cake with chocolate shavings, sprinkles, or even a dusting of cocoa powder for an extra touch.

Enjoy this rich and flavorful Guinness Chocolate Cake!

Leprechaun Pie

Ingredients:

For the Crust:

- 1 1/2 cups graham cracker crumbs
- 1/4 cup granulated sugar
- 1/2 cup unsalted butter, melted

For the Mint Filling:

- 1 package (3.4 oz) instant vanilla pudding mix
- 2 cups whole milk
- 1/2 cup heavy cream
- 1/2 cup sour cream
- 1/4 cup green mint-flavored liqueur (like Creme de Menthe) or 1 teaspoon mint extract (for a non-alcoholic version)
- A few drops of green food coloring (optional)

For the Whipped Cream Topping:

- 1 cup heavy cream
- 2 tablespoons powdered sugar
- 1 teaspoon vanilla extract

Instructions:

1. Prepare the Crust:

- Preheat your oven to 350°F (175°C).
- In a medium bowl, combine graham cracker crumbs, sugar, and melted butter. Mix until the crumbs are evenly coated and the mixture resembles wet sand.
- Press the mixture firmly into the bottom and up the sides of a 9-inch pie dish to form an even crust.
- Bake for 8-10 minutes until set and slightly golden. Allow to cool completely.

2. Prepare the Mint Filling:

- In a large bowl, whisk together the instant vanilla pudding mix and milk until smooth and thickened, about 2 minutes.
- Stir in the sour cream and green mint-flavored liqueur (or mint extract) until well combined. Add a few drops of green food coloring if you want a more vibrant green color.
- Pour the filling into the cooled graham cracker crust and smooth the top with a spatula.

3. Chill:

- Refrigerate the pie for at least 2 hours, or until the filling is set and firm.

4. Prepare the Whipped Cream Topping:

- In a chilled mixing bowl, whip the heavy cream with an electric mixer until it begins to thicken.
- Add the powdered sugar and vanilla extract, and continue whipping until stiff peaks form.
- Spread the whipped cream over the set mint filling or pipe it decoratively.

5. Garnish and Serve:

- Optionally, garnish the whipped cream with chocolate shavings, mint leaves, or green sprinkles.
- Slice and serve chilled.

Tips:

- **Mint Flavor:** Adjust the mint flavor to your liking. If using mint extract, start with 1/2 teaspoon and add more if needed.
- **Food Coloring:** If you want a bright green pie, gel food coloring works best. Add it gradually until you achieve the desired color.
- **Storage:** Store the pie in the refrigerator for up to 3 days. The crust may become a bit softer over time but will still be delicious.

This Leprechaun Pie is a fun and festive way to celebrate St. Patrick's Day with a minty twist! Enjoy!

Mint Chocolate Chip Cookies

Ingredients:

- 1 cup (2 sticks) unsalted butter, softened
- 1 cup granulated sugar
- 1 cup packed brown sugar
- 2 large eggs
- 1 teaspoon vanilla extract
- 1/2 teaspoon peppermint extract
- 2 1/4 cups all-purpose flour
- 1 teaspoon baking soda
- 1/2 teaspoon baking powder
- 1/2 teaspoon salt
- 1 cup mini chocolate chips
- 1/2 cup crushed peppermint candies or candy canes (optional, for extra minty crunch and decoration)

Instructions:

1. Preheat the Oven:

- Preheat your oven to 350°F (175°C). Line baking sheets with parchment paper or silicone baking mats.

2. Cream the Butter and Sugars:

- In a large bowl, beat the softened butter, granulated sugar, and brown sugar together until light and fluffy, about 3-4 minutes.

3. Add Eggs and Extracts:

- Beat in the eggs one at a time, mixing well after each addition. Add the vanilla extract and peppermint extract, mixing until combined.

4. Mix Dry Ingredients:

- In a separate bowl, whisk together the flour, baking soda, baking powder, and salt.

5. Combine Ingredients:

- Gradually add the dry ingredients to the wet ingredients, mixing on low speed until just combined. Be careful not to overmix.

6. Add Chocolate Chips and Peppermint:

- Fold in the mini chocolate chips and crushed peppermint candies, if using.

7. Scoop and Bake:

- Drop rounded tablespoons of dough onto the prepared baking sheets, spacing them about 2 inches apart. If you want a more uniform shape, you can use a cookie scoop.

8. Bake:

- Bake in the preheated oven for 10-12 minutes, or until the edges are lightly golden. The centers may still look slightly soft; that's okay as they will firm up as they cool.

9. Cool:

- Allow the cookies to cool on the baking sheets for about 5 minutes, then transfer them to wire racks to cool completely.

Tips:

- **Mint Extract:** Adjust the amount of peppermint extract to your taste. Peppermint extract is quite strong, so start with 1/2 teaspoon and add more if desired.
- **Peppermint Candies:** If using crushed peppermint candies, they can be added directly to the dough or sprinkled on top of the cookies before baking for added decoration and crunch.
- **Storage:** Store the cookies in an airtight container at room temperature for up to 1 week. You can also freeze the cookies for up to 3 months.

These Mint Chocolate Chip Cookies are a delicious twist on a classic favorite and offer a refreshing minty kick. Enjoy your baking!

Irish Cream Cheesecake

Ingredients:

For the Crust:

- 1 1/2 cups graham cracker crumbs
- 1/4 cup granulated sugar
- 1/2 cup unsalted butter, melted

For the Cheesecake Filling:

- 4 (8 oz each) packages cream cheese, softened
- 1 cup granulated sugar
- 1 teaspoon vanilla extract
- 1/2 cup Irish cream liqueur (like Baileys)
- 3 large eggs
- 1 cup sour cream
- 1 cup heavy cream

For the Whipped Cream Topping:

- 1 cup heavy cream
- 2 tablespoons powdered sugar
- 1 teaspoon vanilla extract

Optional Garnish:

- Chocolate shavings or curls
- Additional Irish cream liqueur drizzle

Instructions:

1. Preheat the Oven:

- Preheat your oven to 325°F (160°C). Grease a 9-inch springform pan or line it with parchment paper.

2. Prepare the Crust:

- In a medium bowl, mix together graham cracker crumbs, granulated sugar, and melted butter until the mixture resembles wet sand.
- Press the mixture firmly into the bottom of the prepared springform pan to form an even layer.
- Bake for 8-10 minutes until set and lightly golden. Let it cool while you prepare the filling.

3. Prepare the Cheesecake Filling:

- In a large mixing bowl, beat the softened cream cheese until smooth and creamy.

- Gradually add the granulated sugar, beating until well combined.
- Beat in the vanilla extract and Irish cream liqueur until fully incorporated.
- Add the eggs one at a time, beating on low speed after each addition. Make sure not to overmix.
- Gently fold in the sour cream and heavy cream until smooth.

4. Bake the Cheesecake:

- Pour the cream cheese filling over the cooled crust in the springform pan.
- Tap the pan gently on the counter to release any air bubbles.
- Bake in the preheated oven for 50-60 minutes, or until the edges are set and the center is slightly jiggly. The center will firm up as it cools.
- Turn off the oven and crack the oven door slightly. Let the cheesecake cool in the oven for 1 hour to prevent cracking.

5. Chill:

- Remove the cheesecake from the oven and refrigerate for at least 4 hours, or overnight, to fully set.

6. Prepare the Whipped Cream Topping:

- In a medium bowl, beat the heavy cream, powdered sugar, and vanilla extract until stiff peaks form.
- Spread or pipe the whipped cream over the chilled cheesecake.

7. Garnish and Serve:

- Optionally, garnish with chocolate shavings or curls and a drizzle of additional Irish cream liqueur.
- Remove the cheesecake from the springform pan and transfer it to a serving platter.

Tips:

- **Crust Variations:** You can use digestive biscuits or Oreos instead of graham crackers for a different flavor.
- **Avoid Cracking:** To help prevent cracking, bake the cheesecake in a water bath (place the springform pan in a larger pan filled with hot water) or ensure that the cheesecake cools gradually.
- **Storage:** Store the cheesecake covered in the refrigerator for up to 1 week. You can also freeze it for up to 3 months.

Enjoy your rich and creamy Irish Cream Cheesecake! It's sure to be a hit at any celebration.

Pot o' Gold Cupcakes

Ingredients:

For the Cupcakes:

- 1 1/2 cups all-purpose flour
- 1 cup granulated sugar
- 1/2 cup unsalted butter, softened
- 2 large eggs
- 1/2 cup milk
- 1/2 cup sour cream
- 1 teaspoon vanilla extract
- 1 1/2 teaspoons baking powder
- 1/2 teaspoon baking soda
- 1/4 teaspoon salt

For the Gold Frosting:

- 1 cup unsalted butter, softened
- 3 cups powdered sugar
- 2 tablespoons heavy cream (or milk)
- 1 teaspoon vanilla extract
- Gold edible glitter or gold-colored sugar (for decoration)

For the Lucky Charm Decoration:

- Rainbow candy or colorful candy pieces (for rainbows)
- Chocolate gold coins or gold-colored candy (for the pot of gold)
- Mini marshmallows (for cloud decorations)

Instructions:

1. Preheat the Oven:

- Preheat your oven to 350°F (175°C). Line a 12-cup muffin tin with cupcake liners.

2. Mix the Dry Ingredients:

- In a medium bowl, whisk together the flour, baking powder, baking soda, and salt.

3. Cream the Butter and Sugar:

- In a large bowl, beat the softened butter and granulated sugar together until light and fluffy, about 3-4 minutes.

4. Add Eggs and Wet Ingredients:

- Beat in the eggs one at a time, mixing well after each addition. Add the vanilla extract and mix until combined.
- Mix in the milk and sour cream until smooth.

5. Combine Dry and Wet Ingredients:

- Gradually add the dry ingredients to the wet ingredients, mixing on low speed until just combined. Be careful not to overmix.

6. Bake the Cupcakes:

- Divide the batter evenly among the cupcake liners, filling each about 2/3 full.
- Bake for 18-20 minutes, or until a toothpick inserted into the center comes out clean.
- Allow the cupcakes to cool in the tin for 5 minutes, then transfer them to a wire rack to cool completely.

7. Prepare the Gold Frosting:

- In a large bowl, beat the softened butter until creamy.
- Gradually add the powdered sugar, beating on low speed until combined. Add the heavy cream (or milk) and vanilla extract, and beat until the frosting is smooth and fluffy.
- Add a few drops of gold food coloring if desired, and mix until well combined. You can also add gold edible glitter or gold-colored sugar for a sparkling effect.

8. Frost the Cupcakes:

- Once the cupcakes are completely cool, frost them with the gold frosting using a piping bag or a spatula.

9. Decorate:

- Decorate each cupcake with rainbow candy or colorful candy pieces to create a rainbow effect. Top with chocolate gold coins or gold-colored candy to represent the pot of gold.
- Add mini marshmallows around the base or on top for cloud decorations.

Tips:

- **Gold Coloring:** For the best gold color, use gel food coloring or gold edible glitter.
- **Decoration Ideas:** Get creative with your decorations! You can use different types of candies to make the pot of gold look as festive as possible.
- **Storage:** Store decorated cupcakes in an airtight container at room temperature for up to 3 days. For longer storage, keep them in the refrigerator.

These Pot o' Gold Cupcakes are sure to be a hit at any celebration with their vibrant colors and delightful decorations!

Green Macarons

Ingredients:

For the Macaron Shells:

- 1 3/4 cups (200g) powdered sugar
- 1 cup (100g) almond flour
- 3 large egg whites
- 1/4 teaspoon cream of tartar
- 1/2 cup (100g) granulated sugar
- Green gel food coloring (about 1/4 teaspoon)
- 1/2 teaspoon vanilla extract (optional)

For the Mint Buttercream Filling:

- 1/2 cup (1 stick) unsalted butter, softened
- 1 1/2 cups powdered sugar
- 1 tablespoon heavy cream (or milk)
- 1/2 teaspoon peppermint extract (adjust to taste)
- A few drops of green food coloring (optional)

Instructions:

1. Prepare the Baking Sheets:

- Line two baking sheets with parchment paper or silicone baking mats. If you have a macaron template, place it under the parchment paper for uniform size.

2. Sift Dry Ingredients:

- In a medium bowl, sift together the powdered sugar and almond flour to remove any lumps.

3. Whip the Egg Whites:

- In a clean, dry bowl, whip the egg whites and cream of tartar using an electric mixer on medium speed until foamy.
- Gradually add the granulated sugar while continuing to whip. Increase to high speed and whip until stiff, glossy peaks form.

4. Add Coloring and Flavoring:

- Add the green gel food coloring to the whipped egg whites. You can add vanilla extract here if using. Gently fold until the color is evenly distributed.

5. Combine with Dry Ingredients:

- Add the sifted almond flour and powdered sugar mixture to the whipped egg whites. Gently fold the mixture with a spatula until combined. Be careful not to overmix. The batter should flow like lava and form a figure-eight without breaking.

6. Pipe the Macarons:

- Transfer the macaron batter to a piping bag fitted with a round tip. Pipe small rounds (about 1.5 inches in diameter) onto the prepared baking sheets, spacing them about 1 inch apart.
- Tap the baking sheets firmly on the counter to release air bubbles and smooth out the tops.

7. Rest the Macarons:

- Let the piped macarons sit at room temperature for about 30-60 minutes, or until a skin forms on the surface. You should be able to lightly touch the tops without the batter sticking to your fingers.

8. Bake the Macarons:

- Preheat your oven to 300°F (150°C). Bake the macarons for 15-18 minutes, or until they are set and have developed a "foot" (a ruffled base). Rotate the baking sheets halfway through baking for even cooking.
- Allow the macarons to cool completely on the baking sheets before removing them.

9. Prepare the Mint Buttercream Filling:

- In a medium bowl, beat the softened butter until creamy.
- Gradually add the powdered sugar, beating on low speed until combined.
- Add the heavy cream and peppermint extract, and beat until the buttercream is light and fluffy. Adjust the peppermint extract to taste and add green food coloring if desired.

10. Assemble the Macarons:

- Pair up the cooled macaron shells of similar sizes. Pipe a small amount of mint buttercream onto the flat side of one shell and top with another shell, pressing gently to spread the filling to the edges.

11. Age the Macarons:

- For the best flavor and texture, let the assembled macarons age in an airtight container in the refrigerator for 24 hours before serving. Bring them to room temperature before enjoying.

Tips:

- **Almond Flour:** Use finely ground almond flour for the best texture. Blanching and grinding your own almonds can also work.
- **Whipping Egg Whites:** Ensure your mixing bowl and beaters are completely clean and free of grease. Use room temperature eggs for better volume.
- **Avoid Cracks:** Proper resting time before baking helps form a skin on the macarons and prevents cracking.

Enjoy making and sharing these beautiful green macarons—they're perfect for adding a touch of elegance and color to your celebrations!

Lucky Charms Rice Krispies Treats

Ingredients:

- **4 cups mini marshmallows**
- **3 tablespoons unsalted butter**
- **6 cups Rice Krispies cereal**
- **3 cups Lucky Charms cereal**
- **1/2 cup additional mini marshmallows (optional, for extra gooeyness)**

Instructions:

1. Prepare the Pan:

- Grease a 9x13 inch baking pan with butter or line it with parchment paper. This will make it easier to lift out the treats later.

2. Melt the Butter and Marshmallows:

- In a large saucepan, melt the butter over medium heat.
- Once melted, add the mini marshmallows and stir continuously until they are completely melted and smooth.

3. Mix in the Cereals:

- Remove the saucepan from the heat.
- Stir in the Rice Krispies cereal until evenly coated with the marshmallow mixture.
- Gently fold in the Lucky Charms cereal until well combined. Be careful not to overmix, as you want to keep the marshmallow coating intact and the marshmallow bits in the Lucky Charms whole.

4. Add Extra Marshmallows (Optional):

- If you like your treats extra gooey, fold in the additional mini marshmallows at this point.

5. Press the Mixture into the Pan:

- Pour the mixture into the prepared baking pan. Use a spatula or wax paper to gently press the mixture evenly into the pan. Pressing too hard can compact the treats and make them less airy.

6. Cool and Cut:

- Allow the treats to cool completely in the pan at room temperature. This will make them easier to cut.
- Once cooled, cut into squares or rectangles.

7. Serve and Enjoy:

- Serve the treats as they are, or package them in festive bags or boxes for gifts or parties.

Tips:

- **Marshmallow Consistency:** For a gooier texture, use a bit more marshmallows. You can also use marshmallow fluff in place of some of the marshmallows if desired.
- **Mixing:** Be gentle when mixing the cereals to avoid crushing the Lucky Charms and losing their shape.
- **Storage:** Store the treats in an airtight container at room temperature for up to 5 days. They can also be frozen for up to 3 months; just make sure they're well wrapped.

These Lucky Charms Rice Krispies Treats are a fun and easy treat that kids and adults alike will enjoy. Perfect for adding a bit of extra magic to your day!

St. Patrick's Day Brownies

Ingredients:

For the Brownies:

- 1/2 cup (1 stick) unsalted butter
- 1 cup granulated sugar
- 2 large eggs
- 1 teaspoon vanilla extract
- 1/3 cup unsweetened cocoa powder
- 1/2 cup all-purpose flour
- 1/4 teaspoon salt
- 1/4 teaspoon baking powder
- 1/2 cup chocolate chips or chunks (optional)

For the Mint Frosting (optional):

- 1/2 cup (1 stick) unsalted butter, softened
- 1 1/2 cups powdered sugar
- 2 tablespoons heavy cream (or milk)
- 1/2 teaspoon mint extract (adjust to taste)
- Green gel food coloring (a few drops, to taste)

For the Garnish (optional):

- Green sprinkles or sugar
- Mini chocolate chips
- Shamrock or St. Patrick's Day-themed decorations

Instructions:

1. Preheat the Oven:

- Preheat your oven to 350°F (175°C). Grease an 8x8 inch baking pan or line it with parchment paper.

2. Melt Butter and Mix Ingredients:

- In a medium saucepan, melt the butter over low heat. Remove from heat and stir in the granulated sugar, eggs, and vanilla extract until well combined.
- Beat in the cocoa powder until smooth.

3. Add Dry Ingredients:

- Stir in the flour, salt, and baking powder until just combined. Avoid overmixing.
- Fold in chocolate chips or chunks if using.

4. Bake the Brownies:

- Pour the batter into the prepared baking pan and spread it evenly.
- Bake for 20-25 minutes, or until a toothpick inserted into the center comes out with a few moist crumbs (not wet batter). The edges should look set and slightly cracked.
- Allow the brownies to cool in the pan on a wire rack before frosting or cutting.

5. Prepare the Mint Frosting (Optional):

- In a medium bowl, beat the softened butter until creamy.
- Gradually add the powdered sugar, beating on low speed until combined.
- Add the heavy cream and mint extract, and beat until the frosting is light and fluffy.
- Add green gel food coloring a few drops at a time until you achieve the desired shade of green.

6. Frost and Garnish:

- Once the brownies are completely cooled, spread the mint frosting evenly over the top.
- Garnish with green sprinkles, mini chocolate chips, or St. Patrick's Day-themed decorations.

7. Serve:

- Cut into squares and serve. Enjoy your festive brownies!

Tips:

- **Consistency:** If you prefer your brownies without frosting, they're still delicious on their own, and you can just add a dusting of powdered sugar or cocoa powder for a simple touch.
- **Mint Flavor:** Adjust the amount of mint extract in the frosting to suit your taste. Mint extract can be quite strong, so start with 1/2 teaspoon and add more if desired.
- **Storage:** Store brownies in an airtight container at room temperature for up to 5 days. They can also be frozen for up to 3 months; just wrap them well to prevent freezer burn.

These St. Patrick's Day Brownies are a delicious way to celebrate and bring a bit of festive cheer to your holiday. Enjoy baking and indulging in these sweet treats!

Irish Apple Cake

Ingredients:

For the Cake:

- 1 1/2 cups all-purpose flour
- 1 teaspoon baking powder
- 1/2 teaspoon baking soda
- 1/2 teaspoon ground cinnamon
- 1/4 teaspoon ground nutmeg
- 1/4 teaspoon salt
- 1/2 cup (1 stick) unsalted butter, softened
- 1/2 cup granulated sugar
- 1/4 cup packed brown sugar
- 1 large egg
- 1/2 cup sour cream or buttermilk
- 2 cups peeled and chopped apples (about 2 medium apples)
- 1/2 cup chopped nuts (optional, such as walnuts or pecans)

For the Glaze (optional):

- 1/2 cup powdered sugar
- 1-2 tablespoons milk or water
- 1/4 teaspoon vanilla extract

Instructions:

1. Preheat the Oven:

- Preheat your oven to 350°F (175°C). Grease and flour an 8-inch round or square cake pan, or line it with parchment paper.

2. Prepare the Dry Ingredients:

- In a medium bowl, whisk together the flour, baking powder, baking soda, cinnamon, nutmeg, and salt.

3. Cream the Butter and Sugars:

- In a large bowl, beat the softened butter, granulated sugar, and brown sugar together until light and fluffy, about 3-4 minutes.

4. Add the Egg and Sour Cream:

- Beat in the egg until well combined.
- Mix in the sour cream (or buttermilk) until smooth.

5. Combine Wet and Dry Ingredients:

- Gradually add the dry ingredients to the wet ingredients, mixing on low speed until just combined.

6. Fold in Apples and Nuts:

- Gently fold in the chopped apples and nuts (if using) until evenly distributed throughout the batter.

7. Bake the Cake:

- Pour the batter into the prepared cake pan and spread it evenly.
- Bake in the preheated oven for 35-40 minutes, or until a toothpick inserted into the center comes out clean.

8. Cool:

- Allow the cake to cool in the pan for 10 minutes, then transfer it to a wire rack to cool completely.

9. Prepare the Glaze (Optional):

- In a small bowl, whisk together the powdered sugar, milk (or water), and vanilla extract until smooth and pourable.
- Drizzle the glaze over the cooled cake or simply dust with powdered sugar if you prefer.

Tips:

- **Apple Variety:** Use a firm, tart apple like Granny Smith for best results. They hold their shape well and add a nice contrast to the sweetness of the cake.
- **Texture:** If you prefer a chunkier texture, you can leave the apples in larger pieces. For a smoother texture, finely chop the apples.
- **Storage:** Store the cake in an airtight container at room temperature for up to 4 days. It can also be frozen for up to 3 months; just wrap it well to prevent freezer burn.

This Irish Apple Cake is a lovely, rustic dessert that pairs wonderfully with a cup of tea or coffee. Enjoy the rich flavors and comforting aroma of this traditional treat!

Green Tea Muffins

Ingredients:

For the Muffins:

- 1 1/2 cups all-purpose flour
- 1/2 cup granulated sugar
- 2 teaspoons baking powder
- 1/2 teaspoon baking soda
- 1/4 teaspoon salt
- 1/2 cup unsalted butter, melted
- 1/2 cup milk
- 2 large eggs
- 2 tablespoons green tea powder (matcha)
- 1 teaspoon vanilla extract

Optional Add-Ins:

- 1/2 cup white chocolate chips
- 1/2 cup chopped nuts (like almonds or walnuts)

For the Topping (optional):

- 2 tablespoons granulated sugar
- 1/2 teaspoon ground cinnamon

Instructions:

1. Preheat the Oven:

- Preheat your oven to 375°F (190°C). Line a 12-cup muffin tin with paper liners or lightly grease the cups.

2. Mix Dry Ingredients:

- In a large bowl, whisk together the flour, sugar, baking powder, baking soda, salt, and green tea powder (matcha).

3. Prepare Wet Ingredients:

- In a separate bowl, whisk together the melted butter, milk, eggs, and vanilla extract until well combined.

4. Combine Wet and Dry Ingredients:

- Add the wet ingredients to the dry ingredients, mixing gently until just combined. Be careful not to overmix; a few lumps are fine.

5. Fold in Optional Add-Ins:

- If using, fold in the white chocolate chips or chopped nuts.

6. Fill Muffin Cups:

- Divide the batter evenly among the 12 muffin cups, filling each about 2/3 full.

7. Add Topping (Optional):

- In a small bowl, mix the granulated sugar and ground cinnamon. Sprinkle this mixture on top of the muffins before baking for a sweet, crunchy topping.

8. Bake:

- Bake in the preheated oven for 18-22 minutes, or until a toothpick inserted into the center comes out clean and the tops are lightly golden.

9. Cool:

- Allow the muffins to cool in the tin for 5 minutes, then transfer them to a wire rack to cool completely.

Tips:

- **Green Tea Powder:** Use high-quality matcha green tea powder for the best flavor. If you only have culinary-grade matcha, that will work too.
- **Flavor Variations:** For a different twist, consider adding lemon zest or a few fresh blueberries to the batter.
- **Storage:** Store the muffins in an airtight container at room temperature for up to 3 days. They can also be frozen for up to 3 months; just wrap them well to prevent freezer burn.

Green Tea Muffins are a lovely way to enjoy the subtle, earthy flavors of green tea in a baked good. They're perfect for adding a touch of elegance to your breakfast or snack time. Enjoy!

Irish Shortbread Cookies

Ingredients:

- 1 cup (2 sticks) unsalted butter, softened
- 1/2 cup granulated sugar
- 2 cups all-purpose flour
- 1/4 teaspoon salt
- 1/2 teaspoon vanilla extract (optional)
- 1/4 cup cornstarch (optional, for extra tenderness)
- Additional sugar for sprinkling (optional)

Instructions:

1. Preheat the Oven:

- Preheat your oven to 350°F (175°C). Line two baking sheets with parchment paper or silicone baking mats.

2. Cream the Butter and Sugar:

- In a large mixing bowl, cream together the softened butter and granulated sugar until light and fluffy. This usually takes about 3-4 minutes.

3. Add Vanilla (Optional):

- If using vanilla extract, mix it into the butter and sugar mixture.

4. Combine Dry Ingredients:

- In a separate bowl, whisk together the flour, salt, and cornstarch (if using). The cornstarch helps create a more tender cookie.

5. Mix Dry and Wet Ingredients:

- Gradually add the dry ingredients to the butter mixture, mixing on low speed until just combined. The dough will be thick and crumbly.

6. Shape the Cookies:

- On a lightly floured surface, roll out the dough to about 1/4-inch thickness. You can also press the dough into a greased or lined 9x9 inch baking pan and cut into squares after baking.
- Cut out cookies using a cookie cutter or into desired shapes with a knife.

7. Transfer to Baking Sheets:

- Place the cut-out cookies onto the prepared baking sheets, spacing them about 1 inch apart.

8. Optional: Sprinkle with Sugar:

- For a little extra sweetness and crunch, sprinkle the tops of the cookies with granulated sugar before baking.

9. Bake:

- Bake in the preheated oven for 12-15 minutes, or until the edges are lightly golden. The centers will still be pale.

10. Cool:

- Allow the cookies to cool on the baking sheets for 5 minutes before transferring them to a wire rack to cool completely.

Tips:

- **Butter:** Ensure the butter is at room temperature for easy creaming and a smooth dough.
- **Texture:** For a more authentic shortbread texture, avoid overworking the dough. It should be crumbly but hold together when pressed.
- **Storage:** Store the cooled cookies in an airtight container at room temperature for up to 1 week. They can also be frozen for up to 3 months; just ensure they are well-wrapped.

These Irish Shortbread Cookies are deliciously simple and perfect for sharing with family and friends. Their buttery richness makes them a delightful treat for any occasion!

Lucky Leprechaun Brownies

Ingredients:

For the Brownies:

- 1/2 cup (1 stick) unsalted butter
- 1 cup granulated sugar
- 2 large eggs
- 1 teaspoon vanilla extract
- 1/3 cup unsweetened cocoa powder
- 1/2 cup all-purpose flour
- 1/4 teaspoon salt
- 1/4 teaspoon baking powder
- 1/2 cup mini chocolate chips or chocolate chunks (optional)

For the Green Frosting (optional):

- 1/2 cup (1 stick) unsalted butter, softened
- 1 1/2 cups powdered sugar
- 2 tablespoons heavy cream (or milk)
- 1/2 teaspoon vanilla extract
- Green gel food coloring

For Decoration:

- Rainbow-colored sprinkles or candy pieces
- Gold edible glitter or gold-colored candy (to represent a pot of gold)
- Shamrock or St. Patrick's Day-themed decorations (optional)

Instructions:

1. Preheat the Oven:

- Preheat your oven to 350°F (175°C). Grease an 8x8 inch baking pan or line it with parchment paper.

2. Melt Butter:

- In a medium saucepan, melt the butter over low heat. Remove from heat and stir in the granulated sugar, eggs, and vanilla extract until well combined.

3. Mix Dry Ingredients:

- Stir in the cocoa powder, flour, salt, and baking powder. Mix until just combined.

4. Add Chocolate Chips (Optional):

- Fold in the mini chocolate chips or chunks if using.

5. Pour Batter into Pan:

- Pour the brownie batter into the prepared baking pan and spread it evenly.

6. Bake:

- Bake in the preheated oven for 20-25 minutes, or until a toothpick inserted into the center comes out with a few moist crumbs (not wet batter). The edges should look set and slightly pulled away from the sides of the pan.

7. Cool:

- Allow the brownies to cool completely in the pan on a wire rack before frosting or cutting.

8. Prepare the Green Frosting (Optional):

- In a medium bowl, beat the softened butter until creamy.
- Gradually add the powdered sugar, beating on low speed until combined.
- Add the heavy cream and vanilla extract, and beat until the frosting is light and fluffy.
- Add green gel food coloring a few drops at a time until you reach the desired shade of green.

9. Frost and Decorate:

- Once the brownies are completely cooled, spread the green frosting evenly over the top.
- Decorate with rainbow-colored sprinkles, gold edible glitter, or candy to represent a pot of gold. You can also use shamrock or other St. Patrick's Day-themed decorations for extra flair.

10. Cut and Serve:

- Cut the brownies into squares and serve. Enjoy your festive treat!

Tips:

- **Frosting:** If you prefer not to frost the brownies, you can dust them with powdered sugar or drizzle with a simple glaze.
- **Decorations:** Get creative with your decorations. You can use various candy or edible decorations to enhance the St. Patrick's Day theme.
- **Storage:** Store the brownies in an airtight container at room temperature for up to 5 days. They can also be frozen for up to 3 months; just wrap them well to prevent freezer burn.

These Lucky Leprechaun Brownies are sure to be a hit with their fudgy texture and festive decorations. Enjoy baking and celebrating!

Green Velvet Whoopie Pies

Ingredients:

For the Green Velvet Cakes:

- 2 1/2 cups all-purpose flour
- 1 1/2 teaspoons baking powder
- 1/2 teaspoon baking soda
- 1/2 teaspoon salt
- 1/2 cup (1 stick) unsalted butter, softened
- 1 cup granulated sugar
- 1 large egg
- 1/2 cup buttermilk
- 1/4 cup vegetable oil
- 1 tablespoon green gel food coloring
- 1 teaspoon vanilla extract
- 1 teaspoon white vinegar

For the Cream Cheese Filling:

- 1/2 cup (1 stick) unsalted butter, softened
- 1/2 cup cream cheese, softened
- 3 cups powdered sugar
- 1 teaspoon vanilla extract
- 2-3 tablespoons heavy cream or milk (if needed)

Instructions:

1. Preheat the Oven:

- Preheat your oven to 350°F (175°C). Line two baking sheets with parchment paper or silicone baking mats.

2. Mix Dry Ingredients:

- In a medium bowl, whisk together the flour, baking powder, baking soda, and salt.

3. Cream Butter and Sugar:

- In a large bowl, beat the softened butter and granulated sugar together until light and fluffy, about 3-4 minutes.

4. Add Wet Ingredients:

- Beat in the egg until fully combined.

- Add the buttermilk, vegetable oil, green gel food coloring, vanilla extract, and white vinegar. Mix until smooth.

5. Combine Wet and Dry Ingredients:

- Gradually add the dry ingredients to the wet ingredients, mixing on low speed until just combined. Be careful not to overmix.

6. Drop Batter onto Baking Sheets:

- Using a cookie scoop or two spoons, drop tablespoon-sized mounds of batter onto the prepared baking sheets, spacing them about 2 inches apart.

7. Bake:

- Bake in the preheated oven for 12-15 minutes, or until the cakes are set and a toothpick inserted into the center comes out clean. The tops should be just starting to crack.

8. Cool:

- Allow the cakes to cool on the baking sheets for 5 minutes before transferring them to a wire rack to cool completely.

9. Prepare the Cream Cheese Filling:

- In a medium bowl, beat the softened butter and cream cheese together until creamy and smooth.
- Gradually add the powdered sugar, beating on low speed until combined.
- Add the vanilla extract and mix until smooth.
- If the filling is too thick, add heavy cream or milk, one tablespoon at a time, until you reach the desired consistency.

10. Assemble the Whoopie Pies:

- Once the cakes are completely cooled, spread or pipe a generous amount of cream cheese filling onto the flat side of one cake.
- Top with another cake, pressing gently to spread the filling to the edges.

11. Serve:

- Serve immediately or store in an airtight container in the refrigerator for up to 3 days. Bring to room temperature before serving if chilled.

Tips:

- **Food Coloring:** Adjust the amount of green gel food coloring to achieve your desired shade of green.

- **Cream Cheese Filling:** Ensure both the butter and cream cheese are softened to make the filling smooth and easy to spread.
- **Texture:** The whoopie pies are best enjoyed fresh, but they can be stored in an airtight container to maintain their softness.

These Green Velvet Whoopie Pies are not only visually appealing with their vibrant color but also deliciously soft and creamy. They're a perfect treat to celebrate any special occasion!

Mint Brownie Cheesecake Bars

Ingredients:

For the Brownie Base:

- 1/2 cup (1 stick) unsalted butter
- 1 cup granulated sugar
- 2 large eggs
- 1 teaspoon vanilla extract
- 1/3 cup unsweetened cocoa powder
- 1/2 cup all-purpose flour
- 1/4 teaspoon salt
- 1/4 teaspoon baking powder
- 1/4 cup peppermint extract (for a stronger mint flavor, optional)

For the Cheesecake Layer:

- 8 oz cream cheese, softened
- 1/2 cup granulated sugar
- 1 large egg
- 1/2 teaspoon vanilla extract
- 1/2 teaspoon peppermint extract
- 1-2 tablespoons green gel food coloring (optional, for a minty green color)

For the Mint Chocolate Ganache:

- 1/2 cup heavy cream
- 1 cup semi-sweet chocolate chips
- 1/2 teaspoon peppermint extract

Instructions:

1. Preheat the Oven:

- Preheat your oven to 350°F (175°C). Grease an 8x8 inch baking pan or line it with parchment paper, leaving an overhang for easy removal.

2. Prepare the Brownie Base:

- In a medium saucepan, melt the butter over low heat. Remove from heat and stir in the granulated sugar until well combined.
- Beat in the eggs and vanilla extract until smooth.
- Stir in the cocoa powder, flour, salt, and baking powder until just combined.
- Add the peppermint extract, if using, for extra mint flavor. Mix well.
- Spread the brownie batter evenly in the prepared pan.

3. Bake the Brownie Base:

- Bake in the preheated oven for 10-12 minutes, until the edges are set but the center is still slightly soft. The brownie layer will continue baking with the cheesecake layer.

4. Prepare the Cheesecake Layer:

- While the brownie base is baking, beat the softened cream cheese in a large bowl until smooth and creamy.
- Add the granulated sugar and mix until combined.
- Beat in the egg, vanilla extract, and peppermint extract until smooth.
- If desired, add green gel food coloring a few drops at a time until you achieve the desired color.

5. Add the Cheesecake Layer:

- After the brownie base has baked for 10-12 minutes, remove it from the oven and spread the cheesecake mixture evenly over the partially baked brownies.

6. Bake the Bars:

- Return the pan to the oven and bake for an additional 20-25 minutes, or until the cheesecake layer is set and the edges are lightly golden.
- Allow the bars to cool in the pan on a wire rack. Once cooled, refrigerate for at least 2 hours or until fully chilled and set.

7. Prepare the Mint Chocolate Ganache:

- In a small saucepan, heat the heavy cream over medium heat until it begins to simmer. Remove from heat.
- Stir in the chocolate chips until smooth and melted.
- Add the peppermint extract and mix until fully combined.

8. Add the Ganache Topping:

- Spread the mint chocolate ganache evenly over the chilled cheesecake layer.
- Refrigerate again for at least 30 minutes to set the ganache.

9. Cut and Serve:

- Once the ganache is set, use the parchment paper overhang to lift the bars out of the pan. Cut into squares or bars.

Tips:

- **Mint Flavor:** Adjust the amount of peppermint extract to suit your taste. Start with a smaller amount and add more if needed.
- **Cheesecake Layer:** Make sure the cheesecake layer is fully chilled before adding the ganache to prevent melting.
- **Storage:** Store the bars in an airtight container in the refrigerator for up to 5 days. They can also be frozen for up to 3 months; just wrap them well to prevent freezer burn.

These Mint Brownie Cheesecake Bars offer a delightful combination of flavors and textures, making them a perfect treat for any occasion. Enjoy!

Irish Cream Brownies

Ingredients:

For the Brownies:

- 1/2 cup (1 stick) unsalted butter
- 1 cup granulated sugar
- 2 large eggs
- 1 teaspoon vanilla extract
- 1/3 cup unsweetened cocoa powder
- 1/2 cup all-purpose flour
- 1/4 teaspoon salt
- 1/4 teaspoon baking powder
- 1/4 cup Irish cream liqueur (like Baileys)

For the Irish Cream Frosting (Optional):

- 1/2 cup (1 stick) unsalted butter, softened
- 1 1/2 cups powdered sugar
- 2 tablespoons Irish cream liqueur
- 1-2 tablespoons heavy cream or milk (if needed)
- 1/4 teaspoon vanilla extract

For the Ganache Topping (Optional):

- 1/2 cup heavy cream
- 1 cup semi-sweet chocolate chips
- 2 tablespoons Irish cream liqueur

Instructions:

1. Preheat the Oven:

- Preheat your oven to 350°F (175°C). Grease an 8x8 inch baking pan or line it with parchment paper, leaving an overhang for easy removal.

2. Prepare the Brownie Batter:

- In a medium saucepan, melt the butter over low heat. Remove from heat and stir in the granulated sugar until well combined.
- Beat in the eggs and vanilla extract until smooth.
- Stir in the cocoa powder, flour, salt, and baking powder until just combined.
- Mix in the Irish cream liqueur until evenly incorporated.

3. Bake the Brownies:

- Pour the brownie batter into the prepared pan and spread it evenly.
- Bake in the preheated oven for 20-25 minutes, or until a toothpick inserted into the center comes out with a few moist crumbs (not wet batter). The edges should look set.

4. Cool:

- Allow the brownies to cool in the pan on a wire rack before adding frosting or ganache.

5. Prepare the Irish Cream Frosting (Optional):

- In a medium bowl, beat the softened butter until creamy.
- Gradually add the powdered sugar, beating on low speed until combined.
- Add the Irish cream liqueur and vanilla extract, and beat until smooth. If the frosting is too thick, add heavy cream or milk one tablespoon at a time until you reach the desired consistency.

6. Frost the Brownies (Optional):

- Once the brownies are completely cooled, spread the Irish cream frosting evenly over the top.

7. Prepare the Ganache Topping (Optional):

- In a small saucepan, heat the heavy cream over medium heat until it begins to simmer. Remove from heat.
- Stir in the chocolate chips until smooth and melted.
- Add the Irish cream liqueur and mix until fully combined.

8. Add the Ganache Topping (Optional):

- Spread or drizzle the ganache over the frosted brownies.
- Refrigerate for at least 30 minutes to set the ganache and frosting.

9. Cut and Serve:

- Once the ganache is set, use the parchment paper overhang to lift the brownies out of the pan. Cut into squares or bars.

Tips:

- **Irish Cream:** For a non-alcoholic option, you can substitute the Irish cream liqueur with a mixture of milk and a few drops of almond or vanilla extract.
- **Cheesecake Layer:** Ensure the brownies are completely cooled before adding frosting or ganache to prevent melting.
- **Storage:** Store the brownies in an airtight container at room temperature for up to 5 days. They can also be frozen for up to 3 months; just make sure they are well-wrapped.

These Irish Cream Brownies are a decadent treat with a rich, creamy flavor that's perfect for any special occasion. Enjoy your indulgent dessert!

Shamrock-shaped Donuts

Ingredients:

- **For the Donuts:**
    - 2 1/4 teaspoons active dry yeast
    - 1/4 cup warm water (110°F)
    - 3/4 cup milk, warmed
    - 1/4 cup granulated sugar
    - 1/4 cup unsalted butter, melted
    - 2 large eggs
    - 3 1/2 cups all-purpose flour
    - 1/2 teaspoon salt
    - Vegetable oil, for frying (if making fried donuts)
- **For the Glaze:**
    - 2 cups powdered sugar
    - 2-3 tablespoons milk
    - 1 teaspoon vanilla extract
    - Green food coloring (optional)

Instructions:

1. **Prepare the Dough:**
    1. In a small bowl, dissolve the yeast in warm water. Let it sit for about 5 minutes, or until it becomes frothy.
    2. In a large mixing bowl, combine the warm milk, sugar, and melted butter. Add the yeast mixture and stir well.
    3. Beat in the eggs, one at a time.
    4. Gradually add the flour and salt, mixing until a dough forms.
    5. Turn the dough out onto a floured surface and knead for about 5 minutes, until smooth and elastic.
    6. Place the dough in a lightly greased bowl, cover with a damp cloth, and let it rise in a warm place for about 1 hour, or until doubled in size.
2. **Shape the Donuts:**
    1. Punch down the dough and turn it out onto a floured surface. Roll out the dough to about 1/2 inch thickness.
    2. Use a shamrock-shaped cookie cutter to cut out the donuts. If you don't have a shamrock cutter, you can use a heart-shaped cutter to make three hearts and then arrange them to form a shamrock shape.
    3. Place the cut donuts on a parchment-lined baking sheet and let them rise for another 30 minutes.
3. **Fry or Bake the Donuts:**
    1. **For Fried Donuts:**
        1. Heat vegetable oil in a deep fryer or large pot to 350°F (175°C).

2. Fry the donuts in batches, being careful not to overcrowd the pot, for about 1-2 minutes per side or until golden brown.
3. Remove with a slotted spoon and drain on paper towels.

2. **For Baked Donuts:**
   1. Preheat your oven to 375°F (190°C).
   2. Place the donuts on a greased baking sheet or in a donut pan.
   3. Bake for 8-10 minutes, or until golden brown.

4. **Glaze the Donuts:**
   1. In a medium bowl, whisk together the powdered sugar, milk, and vanilla extract until smooth. Add green food coloring if desired.
   2. Dip the cooled donuts into the glaze, letting any excess drip off. Allow the glaze to set before serving.

Enjoy your shamrock-shaped donuts! They're perfect for a festive occasion or just for a fun twist on a classic treat.

Guinness Stout Cupcakes

Ingredients:

For the Cupcakes:

- 1 cup (240 ml) Guinness Stout (or other dark stout beer)
- 1 cup (2 sticks) unsalted butter
- 1/2 cup (50 g) unsweetened cocoa powder
- 2 cups (400 g) granulated sugar
- 1 1/2 cups (190 g) all-purpose flour
- 1 1/2 teaspoons baking powder
- 1 1/2 teaspoons baking soda
- 1/2 teaspoon salt
- 2 large eggs
- 1/2 cup (120 ml) sour cream

For the Frosting:

- 1/2 cup (1 stick) unsalted butter, softened
- 4 ounces (115 g) cream cheese, softened
- 3 cups (360 g) powdered sugar
- 2 tablespoons heavy cream (or milk)
- 1/4 cup (60 ml) Irish whiskey (optional)
- 1 teaspoon vanilla extract

Instructions:

1. **Prepare the Cupcakes:**
    1. Preheat your oven to 350°F (175°C). Line a cupcake pan with paper liners.
    2. In a medium saucepan, bring the Guinness Stout to a simmer over medium heat. Add the butter and stir until melted. Remove from heat and whisk in the cocoa powder until smooth. Let the mixture cool slightly.
    3. In a large bowl, whisk together the sugar, flour, baking powder, baking soda, and salt.
    4. In another bowl, beat the eggs until well combined. Mix in the sour cream.
    5. Add the slightly cooled Guinness mixture to the egg mixture, then add the dry ingredients. Stir until just combined; be careful not to overmix.
    6. Divide the batter evenly among the cupcake liners, filling each about 2/3 full.
    7. Bake for 18-22 minutes, or until a toothpick inserted into the center of a cupcake comes out clean.
    8. Let the cupcakes cool in the pan for 5 minutes, then transfer to a wire rack to cool completely.
2. **Make the Frosting:**

1. In a large bowl, beat the butter and cream cheese together until smooth and creamy.
2. Gradually add the powdered sugar, beating until well combined.
3. Add the heavy cream (or milk), Irish whiskey (if using), and vanilla extract. Beat until the frosting is light and fluffy.
4. If the frosting is too thick, add a little more cream or milk; if too thin, add a bit more powdered sugar.

3. **Frost the Cupcakes:**
    1. Once the cupcakes are completely cool, frost them with the cream cheese frosting using a piping bag or a knife.
    2. Optionally, you can garnish with a sprinkle of cocoa powder or some chocolate shavings for extra flair.

Enjoy your Guinness Stout Cupcakes! They pair wonderfully with a cup of coffee or a glass of stout.

Green Pistachio Cake

Ingredients:

For the Cake:

- 1 cup (120 g) shelled pistachios (raw or roasted, unsalted)
- 1 1/2 cups (190 g) all-purpose flour
- 1 teaspoon baking powder
- 1/2 teaspoon baking soda
- 1/2 teaspoon salt
- 1/2 cup (1 stick) unsalted butter, softened
- 1 cup (200 g) granulated sugar
- 3 large eggs
- 1/2 cup (120 ml) sour cream or Greek yogurt
- 1/2 cup (120 ml) whole milk
- 1 teaspoon vanilla extract
- Green food coloring (optional)

For the Frosting:

- 1/2 cup (1 stick) unsalted butter, softened
- 4 ounces (115 g) cream cheese, softened
- 2 cups (240 g) powdered sugar
- 1/2 cup (60 g) finely ground pistachios
- 1 teaspoon vanilla extract
- 1-2 tablespoons milk or cream (as needed)

For Garnish (optional):

- Chopped pistachios
- Edible flowers
- A light dusting of powdered sugar

Instructions:

1. **Prepare the Pistachios:**
    1. Preheat your oven to 350°F (175°C).
    2. Place the pistachios in a food processor and pulse until finely ground. Be careful not to process them too much or they'll turn into paste.
2. **Make the Cake:**
    1. In a medium bowl, whisk together the flour, baking powder, baking soda, and salt.
    2. In a large mixing bowl, cream the butter and sugar together until light and fluffy.
    3. Beat in the eggs, one at a time, mixing well after each addition.
    4. Mix in the vanilla extract.

5. Add the flour mixture in three parts, alternating with the milk and sour cream, beginning and ending with the flour mixture. Mix until just combined.
6. Gently fold in the ground pistachios. Add green food coloring if desired to enhance the color.
7. Divide the batter evenly between two greased and floured 8-inch round cake pans (or one 9x13-inch pan).
8. Bake for 25-30 minutes, or until a toothpick inserted into the center comes out clean.
9. Let the cakes cool in the pans for 10 minutes, then transfer to a wire rack to cool completely.

3. **Make the Frosting:**
   1. In a large bowl, beat the butter and cream cheese until smooth and creamy.
   2. Gradually add the powdered sugar and beat until well combined.
   3. Mix in the finely ground pistachios and vanilla extract.
   4. Add milk or cream as needed to achieve a spreadable consistency.
4. **Assemble and Frost the Cake:**
   1. If you're using two layers, level the cakes with a knife if needed. Place one layer on a serving plate or cake stand.
   2. Spread a layer of frosting on top of the first cake layer, then place the second layer on top.
   3. Frost the top and sides of the cake with the remaining frosting.
   4. Garnish with chopped pistachios, edible flowers, or a light dusting of powdered sugar if desired.

Enjoy your Green Pistachio Cake! It's a delightful and eye-catching dessert that's sure to be a hit.

Lemon and Lime Bars

Ingredients:

For the Crust:

- 1 3/4 cups (220 g) all-purpose flour
- 1/2 cup (100 g) granulated sugar
- 1/4 teaspoon salt
- 1/2 cup (1 stick) unsalted butter, cold and cut into small pieces

For the Filling:

- 1/2 cup (120 ml) fresh lemon juice (about 2 lemons)
- 1/2 cup (120 ml) fresh lime juice (about 3 limes)
- 1 tablespoon lemon zest
- 1 tablespoon lime zest
- 4 large eggs
- 1 1/2 cups (300 g) granulated sugar
- 1/4 cup (30 g) all-purpose flour
- 1/2 teaspoon baking powder
- Powdered sugar, for dusting

Instructions:

1. **Prepare the Crust:**
    1. Preheat your oven to 350°F (175°C). Line a 9x13-inch baking pan with parchment paper, leaving an overhang on the sides for easy removal.
    2. In a medium bowl, whisk together the flour, sugar, and salt.
    3. Cut in the cold butter using a pastry cutter or your fingers until the mixture resembles coarse crumbs.
    4. Press the mixture evenly into the bottom of the prepared pan.
    5. Bake for 15-20 minutes, or until the edges are lightly golden. Remove from the oven and let it cool slightly.
2. **Prepare the Filling:**
    1. In a large bowl, whisk together the lemon juice, lime juice, lemon zest, lime zest, and eggs until well combined.
    2. In another bowl, whisk together the sugar, flour, and baking powder.
    3. Gradually add the dry ingredients to the wet ingredients, whisking until smooth.
3. **Bake the Bars:**
    1. Pour the filling over the pre-baked crust.
    2. Return the pan to the oven and bake for 20-25 minutes, or until the filling is set and the edges are slightly golden.
    3. Remove from the oven and let it cool completely in the pan on a wire rack.
4. **Finish and Serve:**

1. Once cooled, lift the bars out of the pan using the parchment paper overhang and transfer to a cutting board.
2. Dust with powdered sugar before cutting into squares or rectangles.

These Lemon and Lime Bars offer a delightful combination of tart and sweet flavors with a buttery crust that complements the citrusy filling perfectly. Enjoy!

Irish Buttercream Frosting

Ingredients:

- 1 cup (2 sticks) unsalted butter, softened
- 3-4 cups (360-480 g) powdered sugar, sifted
- 2 tablespoons heavy cream (or milk)
- 2 tablespoons Irish whiskey (adjust to taste)
- 1 teaspoon vanilla extract
- A pinch of salt (optional, to taste)

Instructions:

1. **Prepare the Butter:**
    1. In a large mixing bowl, beat the softened butter with an electric mixer on medium speed until creamy and smooth, about 2-3 minutes.
2. **Add Sugar:**
    1. Gradually add the powdered sugar, 1 cup at a time, beating on low speed until combined. Increase the speed to medium and continue to beat until the mixture is light and fluffy.
3. **Add Cream and Flavorings:**
    1. Add the heavy cream (or milk), Irish whiskey, and vanilla extract. Beat on medium speed until well combined. The frosting should be smooth and spreadable.
4. **Adjust Consistency and Flavor:**
    1. If the frosting is too thick, add a little more cream or milk, one teaspoon at a time, until you reach the desired consistency.
    2. If the frosting is too thin, add a bit more powdered sugar to thicken it up.
    3. Taste and add a pinch of salt if needed to balance the sweetness.
5. **Frost Your Cake or Cupcakes:**
    1. Once the frosting is ready, spread it over your cooled cake or cupcakes using a spatula or pipe it with a piping bag for a more decorative touch.

Tips:

- **Chill the Frosting:** If the frosting becomes too soft while working with it, chill it in the refrigerator for about 10-15 minutes, then re-whip it to firm it up.
- **Flavor Variations:** You can adjust the amount of Irish whiskey according to your taste. If you prefer a non-alcoholic version, you can substitute with a splash of milk or a few drops of Irish cream extract.

This Irish Buttercream Frosting adds a delicious, buttery richness to your baked goods with a hint of Irish flair. Enjoy decorating your treats with this smooth and flavorful frosting!

St. Patrick's Day Cheesecake Swirl Brownies

Ingredients:

For the Brownies:

- 1/2 cup (1 stick) unsalted butter
- 1 cup (200 g) granulated sugar
- 2 large eggs
- 1 teaspoon vanilla extract
- 1/3 cup (30 g) unsweetened cocoa powder
- 1/2 cup (65 g) all-purpose flour
- 1/4 teaspoon salt
- 1/4 teaspoon baking powder

For the Cheesecake Swirl:

- 8 ounces (225 g) cream cheese, softened
- 1/4 cup (50 g) granulated sugar
- 1 large egg
- 1/2 teaspoon vanilla extract
- 1-2 tablespoons green food coloring (optional, for festive color)

Instructions:

1. **Preheat Oven and Prepare Pan:**
    1. Preheat your oven to 350°F (175°C).
    2. Line an 8x8-inch (20x20 cm) baking pan with parchment paper, leaving an overhang on the sides for easy removal.
2. **Prepare the Brownie Batter:**
    1. In a medium saucepan, melt the butter over medium heat. Remove from heat and stir in the sugar until well combined.
    2. Beat in the eggs, one at a time, then stir in the vanilla extract.
    3. Mix in the cocoa powder, flour, salt, and baking powder until just combined.
    4. Spread the brownie batter evenly in the prepared pan.
3. **Prepare the Cheesecake Swirl:**
    1. In a medium bowl, beat the softened cream cheese with an electric mixer until smooth and creamy.
    2. Add the sugar, egg, and vanilla extract, and beat until well combined.
    3. If using, add green food coloring to the cheesecake mixture and mix until you achieve the desired color.
4. **Assemble the Brownies:**
    1. Drop spoonfuls of the cheesecake mixture over the brownie batter.
    2. Use a knife or a skewer to gently swirl the cheesecake mixture into the brownie batter. Be careful not to over-swirl; you want a marbled effect.

5. **Bake and Cool:**
    1. Bake in the preheated oven for 30-35 minutes, or until a toothpick inserted into the center comes out with a few moist crumbs.
    2. Let the brownies cool completely in the pan on a wire rack before lifting them out using the parchment paper overhang.
6. **Serve:**
    1. Once cooled, cut into squares and serve.

Optional Garnish:

- You can sprinkle a bit of powdered sugar on top for a touch of elegance.
- For extra festive flair, top with some green sprinkles or edible gold stars.

These St. Patrick's Day Cheesecake Swirl Brownies offer a delicious combination of fudgy brownies and creamy cheesecake with a fun and festive twist. Enjoy!

Green Jello Cupcakes

Ingredients:

For the Cupcakes:

- 1 cup (240 ml) water
- 1 box (3 oz or 85 g) lime-flavored Jello (or any green Jello flavor)
- 1 cup (2 sticks) unsalted butter, softened
- 1 cup (200 g) granulated sugar
- 2 large eggs
- 1 1/2 cups (190 g) all-purpose flour
- 1 1/2 teaspoons baking powder
- 1/4 teaspoon salt

For the Frosting:

- 1/2 cup (1 stick) unsalted butter, softened
- 4 ounces (115 g) cream cheese, softened
- 3-4 cups (360-480 g) powdered sugar, sifted
- 2-3 tablespoons milk or heavy cream
- 1 teaspoon vanilla extract
- Green food coloring (optional, for extra vibrancy)

Instructions:

1. **Prepare the Jello Mixture:**
    1. In a small saucepan, bring the water to a boil. Remove from heat and stir in the lime Jello until completely dissolved. Let it cool to room temperature.
2. **Make the Cupcake Batter:**
    1. Preheat your oven to 350°F (175°C) and line a muffin tin with paper liners.
    2. In a medium bowl, whisk together the flour, baking powder, and salt.
    3. In a large mixing bowl, cream the butter and sugar together until light and fluffy.
    4. Beat in the eggs one at a time, mixing well after each addition.
    5. Gradually add the flour mixture to the butter mixture, alternating with the cooled Jello mixture, beginning and ending with the flour mixture. Mix until just combined.
3. **Bake the Cupcakes:**
    1. Divide the batter evenly among the cupcake liners, filling each about 2/3 full.
    2. Bake for 18-22 minutes, or until a toothpick inserted into the center comes out clean.
    3. Let the cupcakes cool in the tin for 5 minutes, then transfer them to a wire rack to cool completely.
4. **Prepare the Frosting:**

1. In a large bowl, beat the butter and cream cheese together until smooth and creamy.
2. Gradually add the powdered sugar, beating until combined.
3. Mix in the milk or cream, vanilla extract, and a few drops of green food coloring if desired.
4. Beat until the frosting is light and fluffy.

5. **Frost the Cupcakes:**
    1. Once the cupcakes are completely cooled, frost them with the cream cheese frosting using a spatula or piping bag.
    2. Decorate with green sprinkles or other festive toppings if desired.

These Green Jello Cupcakes are not only visually appealing but also delicious with a tangy kick from the lime Jello. They're perfect for adding a bit of fun to any occasion!

Minty Chocolate Fondue

Ingredients:

- 8 ounces (225 g) semisweet or dark chocolate, chopped
- 1 cup (240 ml) heavy cream
- 2 tablespoons unsalted butter
- 1/2 teaspoon peppermint extract (adjust to taste)
- 1 tablespoon sugar (optional, for added sweetness)
- A pinch of salt

For Dipping:

- Fresh strawberries
- Banana slices
- Marshmallows
- Cubed pound cake or brownies
- Pretzels

Instructions:

1. **Prepare the Chocolate Fondue:**
    1. In a medium saucepan, heat the heavy cream over medium heat until it begins to simmer. Do not let it come to a full boil.
    2. Remove the saucepan from the heat and add the chopped chocolate. Let it sit for a few minutes to allow the chocolate to soften.
    3. Gently stir the chocolate and cream together until smooth and fully combined.
    4. Stir in the butter until melted and fully incorporated.
    5. Add the peppermint extract and stir well. Taste and adjust the mint flavor as desired. If you want it sweeter, you can stir in a tablespoon of sugar.
    6. Add a pinch of salt to balance the flavors.
2. **Serve the Fondue:**
    1. Transfer the chocolate fondue to a fondue pot or a heatproof serving bowl. If using a fondue pot, keep it warm over a low flame or candle.
    2. Arrange your dipping items on a platter around the fondue.
3. **Enjoy:**
    1. Use skewers or fondue forks to dip the fruits, marshmallows, cake, or pretzels into the warm, minty chocolate.

Tips:

- **Keeping Warm:** If you don't have a fondue pot, you can keep the chocolate warm in a heatproof bowl over a pot of simmering water (a double boiler). Just make sure the bowl doesn't touch the water.

- **Customization:** You can use milk chocolate or white chocolate instead of dark chocolate if you prefer a different flavor profile.
- **Mint Flavor:** Adjust the amount of peppermint extract based on your taste preference. A little goes a long way.

Minty Chocolate Fondue is a delicious and interactive dessert that's perfect for parties or a cozy night in. Enjoy the rich, chocolatey goodness with a refreshing minty twist!

Shamrock Cheesecake Bites

Ingredients:

For the Crust:

- 1 cup (120 g) graham cracker crumbs
- 1/4 cup (50 g) granulated sugar
- 1/4 cup (60 g) unsalted butter, melted

For the Cheesecake Filling:

- 16 ounces (450 g) cream cheese, softened
- 1/2 cup (100 g) granulated sugar
- 1 teaspoon vanilla extract
- 2 large eggs
- 1/2 cup (120 ml) sour cream
- 1/2 cup (120 ml) heavy cream
- Green food coloring (optional, for festive color)

For the Shamrock Design:

- Green candy melts or green chocolate (optional, for decorating)
- Edible glitter or gold dust (optional, for added flair)

Instructions:

1. **Prepare the Crust:**
    1. Preheat your oven to 325°F (163°C).
    2. Line a mini muffin tin with paper liners or grease it lightly.
    3. In a medium bowl, mix together the graham cracker crumbs, granulated sugar, and melted butter until well combined.
    4. Press about 1 tablespoon of the mixture into the bottom of each muffin cup. Use the back of a spoon or a small tamper to press it down firmly.
    5. Bake the crusts for 5-7 minutes, then remove from the oven and let them cool.
2. **Prepare the Cheesecake Filling:**
    1. In a large bowl, beat the softened cream cheese until smooth and creamy.
    2. Add the granulated sugar and vanilla extract, and beat until well combined.
    3. Add the eggs, one at a time, mixing well after each addition.
    4. Mix in the sour cream and heavy cream until smooth.
    5. If desired, add a few drops of green food coloring to achieve a festive green hue.
3. **Assemble and Bake:**
    1. Spoon or pipe the cheesecake filling on top of the cooled crusts, filling each cup nearly to the top.
    2. Smooth the tops with a spatula.

3. Bake for 15-20 minutes, or until the cheesecakes are set but still slightly jiggly in the center.
4. Turn off the oven and crack the door open, letting the cheesecakes cool in the oven for about 1 hour.
5. Remove the cheesecakes from the oven and let them cool completely at room temperature, then refrigerate for at least 2 hours or until fully chilled.

4. **Decorate:**
    1. If using green candy melts or chocolate, melt according to package instructions and use it to pipe shamrock shapes on top of each cheesecake bite. Alternatively, you can use a shamrock stencil to create the design.
    2. Sprinkle with edible glitter or gold dust for extra festive flair if desired.
5. **Serve:**
    1. Once decorated, keep the cheesecake bites refrigerated until ready to serve.

These Shamrock Cheesecake Bites are a delightful combination of creamy cheesecake and a touch of festive green, making them a perfect treat for any St. Patrick's Day celebration!

Irish Potato Candy

Ingredients:

- 1/2 cup (1 stick) unsalted butter, softened
- 4 cups (450 g) powdered sugar
- 1 cup (120 g) sweetened shredded coconut
- 1/2 cup (120 ml) cream cheese, softened
- 1 teaspoon vanilla extract
- 1 tablespoon ground cinnamon (for coating)
- 1 tablespoon cocoa powder (optional, for coating)

Instructions:

1. **Prepare the Mixture:**
    1. In a large mixing bowl, cream together the softened butter and cream cheese until smooth and well combined.
    2. Gradually add the powdered sugar, mixing on low speed to avoid a mess until fully incorporated. Once all the powdered sugar is added, beat on medium speed until smooth.
    3. Mix in the shredded coconut and vanilla extract until evenly distributed.
2. **Shape the Candy:**
    1. Using your hands or a small cookie scoop, form the mixture into small, potato-shaped balls, about 1 inch (2.5 cm) in size.
    2. Place the shaped candies on a parchment-lined baking sheet or plate.
3. **Coat the Candies:**
    1. In a small bowl, combine the ground cinnamon with the cocoa powder if using.
    2. Roll each candy in the cinnamon (and cocoa powder, if using) mixture until well coated.
    3. Place the coated candies back on the parchment-lined sheet.
4. **Chill:**
    1. Refrigerate the candies for at least 1 hour to firm up before serving.
5. **Serve:**
    1. Once chilled and firm, the candies are ready to enjoy. Store any leftovers in an airtight container in the refrigerator.

Tips:

- **Texture:** If the mixture is too sticky to handle, add a little more powdered sugar. If it's too dry, a small amount of cream cheese or a splash of milk can help achieve the right consistency.
- **Flavor Variations:** For a twist, you can add a bit of finely chopped nuts to the mixture or a dash of your favorite spices.
- **Presentation:** To make them look more like real potatoes, you can use a fork to create small indentations or texture on the surface of the candies before coating them.

These Irish Potato Candies are a fun and whimsical treat that adds a touch of festivity to any occasion, especially St. Patrick's Day. Enjoy your sweet, coconutty bites!

Green Cinnamon Rolls

Ingredients:

For the Dough:

- 1 cup (240 ml) warm milk (110°F or 45°C)
- 1/2 cup (1 stick) unsalted butter, melted
- 1/4 cup (50 g) granulated sugar
- 2 1/4 teaspoons (1 packet) active dry yeast
- 3 1/2 to 4 cups (440-500 g) all-purpose flour
- 1/2 teaspoon salt
- 1 large egg

For the Filling:

- 1/2 cup (1 stick) unsalted butter, softened
- 1 cup (200 g) brown sugar, packed
- 2 tablespoons ground cinnamon

For the Green Glaze:

- 1 cup (120 g) powdered sugar
- 2-3 tablespoons milk or heavy cream
- 1/2 teaspoon vanilla extract
- Green food coloring

Instructions:

1. **Prepare the Dough:**
    1. In a large bowl, combine the warm milk, melted butter, and granulated sugar. Sprinkle the yeast over the top and let it sit for about 5-10 minutes, until it becomes frothy.
    2. Add the egg and salt to the yeast mixture, then gradually mix in 3 1/2 cups of flour, one cup at a time, until a dough forms.
    3. Turn the dough out onto a floured surface and knead for about 5-7 minutes, adding more flour if necessary, until the dough is smooth and elastic.
    4. Place the dough in a lightly greased bowl, cover with a damp cloth or plastic wrap, and let it rise in a warm place for about 1-1.5 hours, or until doubled in size.
2. **Prepare the Filling:**
    1. In a small bowl, mix together the softened butter, brown sugar, and cinnamon until well combined.
3. **Assemble the Cinnamon Rolls:**
    1. Preheat your oven to 350°F (175°C) and grease a 9x13-inch baking dish.
    2. Once the dough has risen, punch it down and turn it out onto a floured surface. Roll it into a rectangle about 1/4 inch thick.

        3. Spread the cinnamon filling evenly over the dough, leaving a small border around the edges.
        4. Roll the dough tightly from one end to the other to form a log.
        5. Slice the log into 12 even pieces and arrange them in the prepared baking dish.
   4. **Bake:**
        1. Cover the rolls with a damp cloth and let them rise for another 30 minutes.
        2. Bake in the preheated oven for 20-25 minutes, or until the rolls are golden brown.
   5. **Prepare the Green Glaze:**
        1. In a medium bowl, whisk together the powdered sugar, 2 tablespoons of milk or cream, and vanilla extract.
        2. Add green food coloring to the glaze until you achieve the desired shade of green. Adjust the consistency by adding more milk or powdered sugar as needed.
   6. **Glaze and Serve:**
        1. Once the cinnamon rolls have cooled slightly, drizzle the green glaze over the top.
        2. Serve warm and enjoy!

Tips:

- **Make Ahead:** You can prepare the rolls the night before and refrigerate them after slicing. In the morning, let them come to room temperature and rise before baking.
- **Variations:** Add chocolate chips or nuts to the filling for extra flavor.
- **Storage:** Store leftover rolls in an airtight container at room temperature for up to 3 days, or freeze for longer storage.

These Green Cinnamon Rolls are sure to be a hit with their festive color and delicious flavor. Enjoy making and sharing this delightful treat!

Irish Whiskey Cake

Ingredients:

For the Cake:

- 1 cup (2 sticks) unsalted butter, softened
- 1 cup (200 g) granulated sugar
- 4 large eggs
- 2 cups (240 g) all-purpose flour
- 1 teaspoon baking powder
- 1/2 teaspoon baking soda
- 1/4 teaspoon salt
- 1/2 cup (120 ml) Irish whiskey
- 1/2 cup (120 ml) milk
- 1 teaspoon vanilla extract
- 1/2 cup (60 g) chopped nuts (optional, such as walnuts or pecans)
- 1/2 cup (80 g) raisins or currants (optional)

For the Whiskey Glaze:

- 1/4 cup (60 ml) Irish whiskey
- 1/4 cup (50 g) granulated sugar

Instructions:

1. **Prepare the Oven and Pan:**
    1. Preheat your oven to 350°F (175°C).
    2. Grease and flour a 9x13-inch baking pan or a Bundt pan.
2. **Make the Cake Batter:**
    1. In a large bowl, cream together the softened butter and sugar until light and fluffy.
    2. Add the eggs one at a time, beating well after each addition.
    3. In a separate bowl, whisk together the flour, baking powder, baking soda, and salt.
    4. Gradually add the dry ingredients to the butter mixture, alternating with the milk and Irish whiskey. Begin and end with the dry ingredients. Mix in the vanilla extract.
    5. If using, fold in the chopped nuts and raisins or currants.
3. **Bake the Cake:**
    1. Pour the batter into the prepared pan and spread it evenly.
    2. Bake for 30-35 minutes (for a 9x13-inch pan) or 45-50 minutes (for a Bundt pan), or until a toothpick inserted into the center comes out clean.
    3. Allow the cake to cool in the pan for about 10 minutes before transferring it to a wire rack to cool completely.
4. **Prepare the Whiskey Glaze:**
    1. In a small saucepan, combine the Irish whiskey and granulated sugar.

2. Heat over medium heat, stirring constantly, until the sugar has dissolved and the mixture is slightly thickened. This should take about 5-7 minutes.
   3. Remove from heat and let it cool slightly.
5. **Glaze the Cake:**
   1. Once the cake has cooled completely, brush or drizzle the whiskey glaze over the cake, allowing it to soak in and glaze the surface.
6. **Serve:**
   1. Slice and serve the cake. It pairs wonderfully with coffee or a glass of Irish whiskey.

Tips:

- **Flavor Enhancements:** For added flavor, consider adding a teaspoon of ground cinnamon or nutmeg to the dry ingredients.
- **Storage:** Store the cake in an airtight container at room temperature for up to 5 days. It also freezes well for up to 3 months.
- **For a Bundt Pan:** If using a Bundt pan, make sure to grease it thoroughly to prevent sticking, and allow extra baking time.

This Irish Whiskey Cake is a deliciously rich and moist treat with a delightful whiskey flavor that's perfect for celebrating St. Patrick's Day or any special occasion. Enjoy!

Matcha Cupcakes

Ingredients:

For the Cupcakes:

- 1 1/2 cups (190 g) all-purpose flour
- 1 cup (200 g) granulated sugar
- 1 1/2 teaspoons baking powder
- 1/2 teaspoon baking soda
- 1/4 teaspoon salt
- 1/2 cup (115 g) unsalted butter, softened
- 2 large eggs
- 1/2 cup (120 ml) milk (whole milk or buttermilk is best)
- 2 tablespoons matcha green tea powder
- 1 teaspoon vanilla extract

For the Matcha Frosting:

- 1 cup (2 sticks) unsalted butter, softened
- 3-4 cups (360-480 g) powdered sugar, sifted
- 2 tablespoons heavy cream (or milk)
- 2 tablespoons matcha green tea powder
- 1 teaspoon vanilla extract

Instructions:

1. **Prepare the Cupcakes:**
    1. Preheat your oven to 350°F (175°C) and line a muffin tin with paper liners.
    2. In a medium bowl, whisk together the flour, sugar, baking powder, baking soda, and salt.
    3. In a large bowl, beat the softened butter until creamy. Add the eggs, one at a time, beating well after each addition.
    4. Mix in the milk, vanilla extract, and matcha powder until well combined.
    5. Gradually add the dry ingredients to the wet ingredients, mixing until just combined. Be careful not to overmix.
2. **Bake the Cupcakes:**
    1. Divide the batter evenly among the cupcake liners, filling each about 2/3 full.
    2. Bake for 18-22 minutes, or until a toothpick inserted into the center comes out clean.
    3. Allow the cupcakes to cool in the tin for 5 minutes, then transfer them to a wire rack to cool completely before frosting.
3. **Prepare the Matcha Frosting:**
    1. In a large bowl, beat the softened butter until smooth and creamy.
    2. Gradually add the powdered sugar, one cup at a time, mixing on low speed until combined. Increase the speed to medium and beat until light and fluffy.

3. Mix in the heavy cream (or milk), matcha powder, and vanilla extract. Beat until the frosting is smooth and well combined. Adjust the consistency by adding more milk or powdered sugar if needed.
4. **Frost the Cupcakes:**
    1. Once the cupcakes are completely cooled, frost them with the matcha frosting using a spatula or a piping bag fitted with your desired tip.
5. **Serve and Enjoy:**
    1. Enjoy the cupcakes immediately or store them in an airtight container at room temperature for up to 3 days.

Tips:

- **Matcha Quality:** Use high-quality culinary grade matcha powder for the best flavor and color. You can find it at specialty tea shops or online.
- **Frosting Consistency:** If the frosting is too thick, add a little more cream or milk. If it's too thin, add more powdered sugar.
- **Decorations:** For a finishing touch, you can sprinkle a little extra matcha powder on top of the frosted cupcakes or garnish with edible flowers.

These Matcha Cupcakes are a wonderful combination of subtle matcha flavor and sweet, fluffy cake. They're perfect for any occasion and are sure to impress with their vibrant green color and unique taste!

Lucky Clover Cake Pops

Ingredients:

For the Cake:

- 1 box (15.25 oz) of vanilla or chocolate cake mix (or homemade equivalent)
- Ingredients needed for cake mix (usually eggs, oil, and water)
- **OR** Use your favorite homemade cake recipe.

For the Frosting:

- 1 cup (240 ml) frosting (store-bought or homemade; vanilla or cream cheese frosting works well)

For the Coating:

- 2 cups (340 g) green candy melts or green chocolate
- 1-2 tablespoons vegetable oil or shortening (optional, for thinning)

For Decoration:

- Green sprinkles (optional)
- Edible glitter or gold dust (optional)

For the Sticks:

- Lollipop sticks or cake pop sticks
- Floral foam or a cake pop stand for drying

Instructions:

1. **Prepare the Cake:**
    1. Bake the cake according to the package directions or your recipe instructions. Allow it to cool completely on a wire rack.
    2. Crumble the cooled cake into a large bowl, breaking it into fine crumbs.
2. **Make the Cake Pop Mixture:**
    1. Add the frosting to the cake crumbs a little at a time, mixing until the mixture is moist and holds together when pressed. You may not need all the frosting; add just enough until the mixture holds together well.
3. **Shape the Cake Pops:**
    1. Use a cookie scoop or your hands to form the cake mixture into small balls (about 1 inch in diameter).
    2. Place the cake balls on a parchment-lined baking sheet.
4. **Shape into Clover:**
    1. To create the clover shape, press four cake balls together to form a clover with four petals. You can use your fingers to gently shape and smooth the edges.

        2. Insert a lollipop stick into each clover shape, pressing it in about halfway. Make sure the stick is secure and doesn't come loose.
 5. **Chill the Cake Pops:**
        1. Place the cake pops in the refrigerator or freezer for about 30 minutes to 1 hour, or until firm.
 6. **Prepare the Coating:**
        1. Melt the green candy melts or chocolate according to the package instructions. If using candy melts, you can add 1-2 tablespoons of vegetable oil or shortening to thin the coating if necessary.
        2. Dip each cake pop into the melted coating, making sure to cover it completely. Gently tap off any excess coating.
 7. **Decorate:**
        1. If desired, sprinkle the wet coating with green sprinkles or edible glitter while it's still soft.
        2. Insert the cake pop sticks into floral foam or a cake pop stand to let the coating set and harden completely.
 8. **Serve:**
        1. Once the coating has set, the Lucky Clover Cake Pops are ready to enjoy! Store them in an airtight container at room temperature for up to 1 week or in the refrigerator for up to 2 weeks.

Tips:

- **Flavor Variations:** You can flavor the cake and frosting with extracts (like mint or almond) to match the theme or to add an extra layer of flavor.
- **Consistency:** If the cake pop mixture is too dry, add a bit more frosting. If it's too wet, add more cake crumbs.
- **Handling:** Keep the cake pops chilled as you work with them to prevent them from becoming too soft and falling off the sticks.

These Lucky Clover Cake Pops are not only visually appealing but also a delicious treat that adds a touch of luck and charm to your celebration. Enjoy crafting these festive and tasty little treats!

Shamrock Cream Puffs

Ingredients:

For the Choux Pastry:

- 1/2 cup (115 g) unsalted butter
- 1 cup (240 ml) water
- 1/4 teaspoon salt
- 1 cup (120 g) all-purpose flour
- 4 large eggs

For the Shamrock Cream Filling:

- 1 cup (240 ml) heavy cream
- 1/2 cup (120 ml) whole milk
- 1/2 cup (100 g) granulated sugar
- 2 tablespoons matcha green tea powder (for color and flavor)
- 1 teaspoon vanilla extract
- 1 tablespoon cornstarch

For the Glaze (Optional):

- 1 cup (120 g) powdered sugar
- 2-3 tablespoons milk
- Green food coloring

Instructions:

1. **Prepare the Choux Pastry:**
    1. Preheat your oven to 375°F (190°C) and line a baking sheet with parchment paper.
    2. In a medium saucepan, combine the butter, water, and salt. Bring to a boil over medium heat.
    3. Once the mixture is boiling, add the flour all at once and stir vigorously with a wooden spoon until the dough pulls away from the sides of the pan and forms a ball.
    4. Remove the pan from heat and let the dough cool for 5 minutes.
    5. Add the eggs one at a time, beating well after each addition until the dough is smooth and shiny.
    6. Transfer the dough to a piping bag fitted with a large round tip. Pipe small mounds of dough onto the prepared baking sheet, spacing them about 2 inches apart.
    7. Bake for 20-25 minutes, or until the puffs are golden brown and puffed up. Turn off the oven and crack the oven door slightly, letting the puffs cool inside for about 10 minutes.
    8. Remove from the oven and let the puffs cool completely on a wire rack.
2. **Prepare the Shamrock Cream Filling:**

1. In a medium bowl, whisk together the milk, heavy cream, sugar, matcha powder, and vanilla extract.
2. In a small saucepan, heat a small portion of the milk mixture with the cornstarch until it begins to thicken, stirring constantly. This should take about 2 minutes.
3. Remove from heat and let it cool slightly before mixing it back into the rest of the milk mixture.
4. Chill the mixture in the refrigerator until it's cold and thickened, about 1 hour.
5. Once chilled, beat the mixture with a hand mixer or stand mixer until it forms stiff peaks.

3. **Assemble the Cream Puffs:**
    1. Once the cream puffs are completely cooled, cut them in half horizontally.
    2. Pipe or spoon the shamrock cream filling onto the bottom half of each puff.
    3. Place the top half of the puff over the filling to sandwich it.
4. **Prepare the Glaze (Optional):**
    1. In a small bowl, mix the powdered sugar with 2-3 tablespoons of milk and a few drops of green food coloring until you achieve a smooth, pourable consistency.
    2. Drizzle or dip the tops of the cream puffs in the green glaze and let it set.
5. **Serve:**
    1. Arrange the Shamrock Cream Puffs on a platter and enjoy!

Tips:

- **Consistency:** If the choux pastry dough is too thick, add an extra egg. If it's too thin, add a bit more flour.
- **Filling Flavor:** Adjust the amount of matcha powder based on your taste preference. If you prefer a stronger green tea flavor, add a bit more matcha.
- **Decorations:** For an extra festive touch, use green sugar crystals or edible glitter on the glazed puffs.

Shamrock Cream Puffs are a delightful and elegant treat that will add a touch of charm and sophistication to your St. Patrick's Day celebrations. Enjoy making and sharing these delicious pastries!

Green Tea and White Chocolate Cookies

Ingredients:

- 2 1/4 cups (280 g) all-purpose flour
- 1/2 teaspoon baking powder
- 1/2 teaspoon baking soda
- 1/4 teaspoon salt
- 1/2 cup (115 g) unsalted butter, softened
- 1/2 cup (100 g) granulated sugar
- 1/2 cup (110 g) packed brown sugar
- 1 large egg
- 1 teaspoon vanilla extract
- 1 tablespoon matcha green tea powder
- 1 cup (170 g) white chocolate chips or chunks

Instructions:

1. **Prepare the Oven:**
    1. Preheat your oven to 350°F (175°C).
    2. Line a baking sheet with parchment paper or a silicone baking mat.
2. **Mix Dry Ingredients:**
    1. In a medium bowl, whisk together the flour, baking powder, baking soda, salt, and matcha green tea powder. Set aside.
3. **Cream Butter and Sugars:**
    1. In a large bowl, using an electric mixer, cream together the softened butter, granulated sugar, and brown sugar until light and fluffy.
4. **Add Wet Ingredients:**
    1. Beat in the egg and vanilla extract until well combined.
5. **Combine Dry and Wet Ingredients:**
    1. Gradually add the dry ingredients to the butter mixture, mixing on low speed until just combined.
6. **Add White Chocolate Chips:**
    1. Fold in the white chocolate chips or chunks with a spatula until evenly distributed throughout the dough.
7. **Shape the Cookies:**
    1. Scoop tablespoons of dough and roll them into balls. Place them on the prepared baking sheet, spacing them about 2 inches apart.
    2. Flatten each dough ball slightly with the palm of your hand or the bottom of a glass.
8. **Bake:**
    1. Bake in the preheated oven for 10-12 minutes, or until the edges are lightly golden. The centers may look slightly underbaked, but they will set as they cool.
    2. Allow the cookies to cool on the baking sheet for about 5 minutes before transferring them to a wire rack to cool completely.
9. **Serve:**

1. Enjoy the cookies once they are completely cooled. Store any leftovers in an airtight container at room temperature for up to 1 week.

Tips:

- **Matcha Quality:** Use high-quality culinary grade matcha powder for the best flavor and color. You can find it at specialty tea shops or online.
- **Butter:** Make sure the butter is softened but not melted for the best texture.
- **Mix-Ins:** Feel free to add other mix-ins such as chopped nuts or dried fruit if desired.

These Green Tea and White Chocolate Cookies are a delicious combination of flavors and textures, offering a unique twist on traditional cookies. Enjoy baking and savoring these delightful treats!

St. Patrick's Day Tiramisu

Ingredients:

For the Cream Mixture:

- 1 cup (240 ml) heavy cream
- 8 oz (225 g) mascarpone cheese, softened
- 1/2 cup (100 g) granulated sugar
- 1/2 cup (120 ml) Bailey's Irish Cream or Irish whiskey
- 1 teaspoon vanilla extract
- 1 tablespoon matcha green tea powder (optional, for color and flavor)

For the Ladyfingers:

- 24-30 ladyfingers (savoiardi)
- 1 cup (240 ml) strong brewed coffee, cooled
- 1/4 cup (60 ml) Bailey's Irish Cream or Irish whiskey (or a mix of both)

For Garnish:

- Cocoa powder or green matcha powder for dusting
- Chocolate shavings or green sprinkles (optional)

Instructions:

1. **Prepare the Cream Mixture:**
    1. In a large bowl, use an electric mixer to whip the heavy cream until stiff peaks form.
    2. In another bowl, combine the mascarpone cheese, granulated sugar, and Bailey's Irish Cream (or Irish whiskey). Mix until smooth and well combined.
    3. Gently fold the whipped cream into the mascarpone mixture until fully incorporated.
    4. If using, mix in the matcha green tea powder until the cream is evenly tinted green.
2. **Prepare the Coffee Mixture:**
    1. In a shallow dish, combine the cooled coffee and Bailey's Irish Cream (or Irish whiskey).
3. **Assemble the Tiramisu:**
    1. Briefly dip each ladyfinger into the coffee mixture, ensuring they are soaked but not overly soggy. Arrange a layer of dipped ladyfingers in the bottom of a 9x9-inch (23x23 cm) baking dish or a similar-sized trifle dish.
    2. Spread half of the mascarpone cream mixture over the ladyfingers, smoothing it out evenly.
    3. Add another layer of dipped ladyfingers on top of the cream layer.
    4. Spread the remaining mascarpone cream mixture over the second layer of ladyfingers.
4. **Chill and Set:**

1. Cover the dish with plastic wrap and refrigerate for at least 4 hours or overnight to allow the flavors to meld and the tiramisu to set.
5. **Garnish and Serve:**
   1. Before serving, dust the top with cocoa powder or matcha powder.
   2. Optionally, garnish with chocolate shavings or green sprinkles for a festive touch.

Tips:

- **Ladyfinger Soaking:** Be quick when dipping the ladyfingers to avoid them becoming too soggy. A brief dip is usually sufficient.
- **Flavor Variations:** You can adjust the amount of Bailey's or Irish whiskey based on your preference for alcohol content.
- **Serving:** Tiramisu is best served chilled and can be made up to 2 days in advance. It's a great make-ahead dessert for parties and gatherings.

This St. Patrick's Day Tiramisu adds a festive green touch to a beloved classic dessert, making it a perfect treat for celebrating the holiday. Enjoy your creamy, delicious tiramisu with a hint of Irish charm!

Chocolate Mint Poke Cake

Ingredients:

For the Cake:

- 1 box (15.25 oz) chocolate cake mix (or use your favorite homemade chocolate cake recipe)
- Ingredients needed for cake mix (usually eggs, oil, and water)
- 1 cup (240 ml) water
- 1/2 cup (120 ml) vegetable oil
- 3 large eggs

For the Mint Filling:

- 1 cup (240 ml) milk
- 1 package (3.4 oz) instant chocolate pudding mix
- 1/2 cup (120 ml) heavy cream
- 1 teaspoon peppermint extract
- Green food coloring (optional)

For the Chocolate Ganache:

- 1 cup (170 g) semi-sweet chocolate chips
- 1/2 cup (120 ml) heavy cream

For Garnish (Optional):

- Whipped cream
- Mint leaves
- Chocolate shavings or sprinkles

Instructions:

1. **Prepare the Cake:**
    1. Preheat your oven to 350°F (175°C) and grease a 9x13-inch baking pan.
    2. In a large bowl, mix the chocolate cake mix, water, vegetable oil, and eggs until well combined.
    3. Pour the batter into the prepared pan and bake according to the package instructions (usually about 30-35 minutes), or until a toothpick inserted into the center comes out clean.
    4. Allow the cake to cool in the pan for about 10 minutes, then use a fork to poke holes all over the cake, about 1 inch apart.
2. **Prepare the Mint Filling:**
    1. In a medium bowl, whisk together the instant chocolate pudding mix and milk until smooth and thickened. Let it sit for about 2 minutes.
    2. In a separate bowl, whip the heavy cream until stiff peaks form. Fold the whipped cream into the pudding mixture until well combined.
    3. Add peppermint extract and a few drops of green food coloring (if using) to the mixture and fold gently until evenly distributed.

3. **Assemble the Cake:**
    1. Spread the mint filling evenly over the cooled cake, making sure it gets into the holes you poked. Smooth it out with a spatula.
    2. Refrigerate the cake for at least 1 hour to let the filling set.
4. **Prepare the Chocolate Ganache:**
    1. In a small saucepan, heat the heavy cream over medium heat until it begins to simmer. Remove from heat.
    2. Add the chocolate chips to the cream and let them sit for about 2 minutes. Stir until the chocolate is completely melted and the ganache is smooth.
    3. Allow the ganache to cool slightly before spreading it over the chilled cake.
5. **Garnish and Serve:**
    1. Spread the chocolate ganache evenly over the mint filling.
    2. Optionally, top with whipped cream, mint leaves, and chocolate shavings or sprinkles for decoration.
    3. Slice and serve chilled.

Tips:

- **Mint Flavor:** Adjust the amount of peppermint extract to your taste. If you prefer a milder mint flavor, use less extract.
- **Food Coloring:** Green food coloring is optional, but it adds a festive touch. Adjust the amount based on your color preference.
- **Storage:** Store leftover cake in an airtight container in the refrigerator for up to 4-5 days.

This Chocolate Mint Poke Cake is a delicious combination of rich chocolate and refreshing mint, perfect for any occasion. Enjoy making and sharing this delectable dessert!

Irish Soda Bread Muffins

Ingredients:

- 2 cups (240 g) all-purpose flour
- 1/2 cup (60 g) whole wheat flour (optional, for a heartier texture)
- 1/4 cup (50 g) granulated sugar
- 1 teaspoon baking soda
- 1/2 teaspoon salt
- 1 cup (240 ml) buttermilk (or make your own with milk and lemon juice)
- 1/4 cup (60 ml) melted unsalted butter
- 1 large egg
- 1 cup (150 g) raisins or currants (optional)
- 1/2 cup (60 g) chopped nuts (optional, such as walnuts or pecans)

For the Topping (Optional):

- 1 tablespoon coarse sugar (for sprinkling on top)

Instructions:

1. **Prepare the Oven:**
   1. Preheat your oven to 375°F (190°C).
   2. Line a muffin tin with paper liners or lightly grease it.
2. **Mix Dry Ingredients:**
   1. In a large bowl, whisk together the all-purpose flour, whole wheat flour (if using), granulated sugar, baking soda, and salt.
3. **Combine Wet Ingredients:**
   1. In a separate bowl, whisk together the buttermilk, melted butter, and egg until well combined.
4. **Combine Dry and Wet Ingredients:**
   1. Pour the wet ingredients into the dry ingredients and stir gently until just combined. Be careful not to overmix; the batter should be slightly lumpy.
   2. Fold in the raisins or currants and chopped nuts (if using).
5. **Fill Muffin Tin:**
   1. Divide the batter evenly among the muffin cups, filling each about 2/3 full.
   2. If desired, sprinkle the tops with coarse sugar for a bit of extra sweetness and texture.
6. **Bake:**
   1. Bake in the preheated oven for 18-22 minutes, or until the muffins are golden brown and a toothpick inserted into the center comes out clean.
   2. Allow the muffins to cool in the tin for 5 minutes before transferring them to a wire rack to cool completely.
7. **Serve:**
   1. Enjoy the muffins warm or at room temperature. They're great with a pat of butter or a dollop of jam.

Tips:

- **Buttermilk Substitute:** If you don't have buttermilk, you can make your own by adding 1 tablespoon of lemon juice or white vinegar to 1 cup of milk. Let it sit for 5 minutes before using.
- **Mix-Ins:** Feel free to experiment with other mix-ins like chopped dried fruit, chocolate chips, or even a bit of grated cheese.
- **Storage:** Store any leftover muffins in an airtight container at room temperature for up to 3 days, or freeze for up to 3 months.

These Irish Soda Bread Muffins offer the traditional flavor of Irish soda bread in a convenient muffin form, making them a perfect addition to your St. Patrick's Day festivities or any day you crave a hearty, comforting treat. Enjoy!

Green Coconut Macaroons

Ingredients:

- 2 1/2 cups (200 g) sweetened shredded coconut

- 1 cup (200 g) granulated sugar
- 1/4 cup (30 g) all-purpose flour
- 1/4 teaspoon salt
- 4 large egg whites
- 1/2 teaspoon vanilla extract
- 1/2 teaspoon peppermint extract (optional, for a minty flavor)
- Green food coloring (gel or liquid)
- 1 cup (170 g) semi-sweet chocolate chips (optional, for dipping)

Instructions:

1. **Prepare the Oven:**
    1. Preheat your oven to 325°F (165°C).
    2. Line a baking sheet with parchment paper or a silicone baking mat.
2. **Mix Dry Ingredients:**
    1. In a large bowl, combine the sweetened shredded coconut, granulated sugar, flour, and salt. Mix well.
3. **Prepare the Egg Whites:**
    1. In a separate, clean bowl, beat the egg whites with an electric mixer until stiff peaks form. This usually takes about 3-4 minutes.
4. **Combine Ingredients:**
    1. Gently fold the egg whites into the coconut mixture until fully combined. Be careful not to deflate the egg whites.
    2. Stir in the vanilla extract, peppermint extract (if using), and a few drops of green food coloring until the desired color is achieved. If you prefer a more intense green color, add more food coloring as needed.
5. **Shape the Macaroons:**
    1. Use a small cookie scoop or tablespoon to drop rounded mounds of the mixture onto the prepared baking sheet. Space them about 1 inch apart.
6. **Bake:**
    1. Bake in the preheated oven for 15-20 minutes, or until the edges are golden brown and the centers are set.
    2. Allow the macaroons to cool on the baking sheet for about 5 minutes before transferring them to a wire rack to cool completely.
7. **Optional: Dip in Chocolate:**
    1. If desired, melt the chocolate chips in a microwave-safe bowl in 30-second intervals, stirring until smooth.
    2. Dip the bottom of each macaroon into the melted chocolate, then place them back on the parchment-lined baking sheet.
    3. Allow the chocolate to set before serving. You can speed up the process by refrigerating the macaroons for about 15 minutes.
8. **Serve:**
    1. Enjoy the macaroons once the chocolate has set. Store any leftovers in an airtight container at room temperature for up to 1 week.

Tips:

- **Coconut Texture:** Ensure you use sweetened shredded coconut for the right texture and sweetness. You can use unsweetened coconut, but you may need to adjust the sugar in the recipe.
- **Coloring:** Gel food coloring is preferable for achieving a vibrant green without adding extra liquid to the mixture.
- **Egg Whites:** Make sure there is no trace of yolk in the egg whites, and the mixing bowl is clean and dry to achieve stiff peaks.

These Green Coconut Macaroons are not only festive but also incredibly easy to make. They offer a delightful combination of chewy coconut with a touch of sweetness, making them a perfect treat for any special occasion. Enjoy!

Guinness and Chocolate Cupcakes

Ingredients:

For the Cupcakes:

- 1 cup (240 ml) Guinness stout (or any dark stout beer)
- 1 cup (230 g) unsalted butter
- 1 cup (200 g) granulated sugar
- 1 cup (220 g) packed brown sugar
- 3/4 cup (65 g) unsweetened cocoa powder
- 1 1/2 cups (190 g) all-purpose flour
- 1 1/2 teaspoons baking powder
- 1 1/2 teaspoons baking soda
- 1/2 teaspoon salt
- 2 large eggs
- 1/2 cup (120 ml) sour cream

For the Cream Cheese Frosting:

- 8 oz (225 g) cream cheese, softened
- 1/2 cup (115 g) unsalted butter, softened
- 3-4 cups (360-480 g) powdered sugar (adjust to desired sweetness)
- 1 teaspoon vanilla extract

Instructions:

1. **Prepare the Oven:**
    1. Preheat your oven to 350°F (175°C).
    2. Line a muffin tin with cupcake liners.
2. **Prepare the Cupcake Batter:**
    1. In a medium saucepan, combine the Guinness stout and butter. Heat over medium heat until the butter is melted. Remove from heat and whisk in the cocoa powder until smooth.
    2. In a large bowl, whisk together the granulated sugar, brown sugar, flour, baking powder, baking soda, and salt.
    3. In a separate bowl, whisk together the eggs and sour cream until well combined.
    4. Pour the Guinness and butter mixture into the dry ingredients and stir until just combined.
    5. Fold in the egg mixture until smooth.
    6. Divide the batter evenly among the cupcake liners, filling each about 2/3 full.
3. **Bake:**
    1. Bake in the preheated oven for 18-22 minutes, or until a toothpick inserted into the center of a cupcake comes out clean.
    2. Allow the cupcakes to cool in the tin for 5 minutes, then transfer them to a wire rack to cool completely.
4. **Prepare the Cream Cheese Frosting:**
    1. In a large bowl, beat the cream cheese and butter together until smooth and creamy.
    2. Gradually add the powdered sugar, one cup at a time, beating well after each addition until the frosting reaches your desired sweetness and consistency.

3. Beat in the vanilla extract.
5. **Frost the Cupcakes:**
   1. Once the cupcakes are completely cool, frost them with the cream cheese frosting using a piping bag or a spatula.
6. **Serve:**
   1. Enjoy the cupcakes immediately, or store them in an airtight container in the refrigerator for up to 3 days.

Tips:

- **Guinness Substitution:** If you prefer not to use alcohol, you can substitute the Guinness with a non-alcoholic stout or another dark beer.
- **Frosting Variations:** For a different twist, you can add a bit of cocoa powder to the cream cheese frosting for a chocolate cream cheese frosting or a touch of Irish whiskey for added flavor.
- **Texture:** Make sure the cupcakes are completely cool before frosting to prevent the frosting from melting.

These Guinness and Chocolate Cupcakes are rich, flavorful, and perfect for celebrating St. Patrick's Day or any occasion that calls for a touch of indulgence. Enjoy baking and savoring these delicious treats!

Shamrock Cake Roll

Ingredients:

For the Cake:

- 3 large eggs

- 1/2 cup (100 g) granulated sugar
- 1/2 cup (60 g) all-purpose flour
- 1/4 teaspoon baking powder
- 1/4 teaspoon salt
- 2 tablespoons unsalted butter, melted
- 1/2 teaspoon vanilla extract
- Green food coloring (gel or liquid)

For the Filling:

- 1 cup (240 ml) heavy cream
- 1/4 cup (50 g) granulated sugar
- 1/2 teaspoon vanilla extract

For the Frosting:

- 1 cup (225 g) cream cheese, softened
- 1/2 cup (115 g) unsalted butter, softened
- 3-4 cups (360-480 g) powdered sugar (adjust to taste)
- 1 teaspoon vanilla extract

Instructions:

1. **Prepare the Cake:**
   - **Preheat the Oven:**
     - Preheat your oven to 350°F (175°C).
     - Line a 15x10-inch jelly roll pan with parchment paper, leaving an overhang on the sides.
   - **Make the Shamrock Design:**
     - In a small bowl, mix a small portion of the cake batter with green food coloring.
     - Transfer this green batter into a piping bag or a plastic bag with a small corner cut off.
     - Pipe shamrock shapes or other designs onto the parchment paper. This will be the decorative layer that's visible when you roll the cake.
   - **Prepare the Cake Batter:**
     - In a medium bowl, beat the eggs and granulated sugar with an electric mixer until thick and pale.
     - Sift the flour, baking powder, and salt into a separate bowl.
     - Gently fold the dry ingredients into the egg mixture, being careful not to deflate it.
     - Fold in the melted butter and vanilla extract.
   - **Bake the Cake:**
     - Pour the plain batter over the shamrock designs on the parchment paper, spreading it evenly.

- Bake in the preheated oven for 10-12 minutes, or until the cake springs back when lightly touched.
  - **Roll the Cake:**
    - While the cake is still warm, invert it onto a clean kitchen towel dusted with powdered sugar.
    - Gently peel away the parchment paper.
    - Starting from one end, roll the cake up with the towel, creating a spiral shape.
    - Let it cool completely while rolled up.
2. **Prepare the Filling:**
   - In a large bowl, beat the heavy cream, granulated sugar, and vanilla extract until stiff peaks form.
3. **Prepare the Frosting:**
   - In a medium bowl, beat the cream cheese and butter until smooth.
   - Gradually add the powdered sugar, one cup at a time, beating well after each addition.
   - Mix in the vanilla extract.
4. **Assemble the Cake Roll:**
   - Unroll the cooled cake carefully and spread the whipped cream filling evenly over the surface.
   - Re-roll the cake without the towel, creating a spiral with the filling inside.
5. **Frost and Decorate:**
   - Spread the cream cheese frosting evenly over the surface of the rolled cake.
   - Optionally, garnish with additional shamrock decorations or edible green sprinkles.
6. **Serve:**
   - Chill the cake roll for at least 1 hour before slicing to help it hold its shape.
   - Slice and serve.

Tips:

- **Shamrock Design:** If you're not confident in piping, you can use a stencil to create the shamrock pattern.
- **Rolling Technique:** Roll the cake gently and evenly to avoid cracking. If it cracks, don't worry; you can cover it with frosting or decorative elements.
- **Storage:** Store the cake roll in the refrigerator for up to 3 days.

This Shamrock Cake Roll is a beautiful and festive way to celebrate St. Patrick's Day with a touch of elegance and fun. Enjoy making and sharing this delightful treat!

Irish Brown Bread Muffins

Ingredients:

- 1 cup (120 g) whole wheat flour
- 1 cup (120 g) all-purpose flour
- 1/2 cup (100 g) granulated sugar
- 1 tablespoon baking powder
- 1/2 teaspoon baking soda

- 1/2 teaspoon salt
- 1/2 cup (115 g) unsalted butter, melted
- 1 cup (240 ml) buttermilk (or make your own with milk and lemon juice)
- 1 large egg
- 1/2 cup (60 g) rolled oats (optional, for added texture)
- 1/2 cup (80 g) raisins or currants (optional)
- 1 tablespoon honey (optional, for extra sweetness)

Instructions:

1. **Prepare the Oven:**
   1. Preheat your oven to 375°F (190°C).
   2. Line a muffin tin with paper liners or lightly grease it.
2. **Mix Dry Ingredients:**
   1. In a large bowl, whisk together the whole wheat flour, all-purpose flour, granulated sugar, baking powder, baking soda, and salt.
3. **Prepare Wet Ingredients:**
   1. In another bowl, whisk together the melted butter, buttermilk, and egg until well combined.
   2. If using honey, mix it into the wet ingredients.
4. **Combine Wet and Dry Ingredients:**
   1. Pour the wet ingredients into the dry ingredients and stir gently until just combined. The batter should be slightly lumpy; do not overmix.
   2. Fold in the rolled oats and raisins or currants if using.
5. **Fill Muffin Tin:**
   1. Divide the batter evenly among the muffin cups, filling each about 2/3 full.
6. **Bake:**
   1. Bake in the preheated oven for 18-22 minutes, or until the tops are golden brown and a toothpick inserted into the center comes out clean.
   2. Allow the muffins to cool in the tin for about 5 minutes before transferring them to a wire rack to cool completely.
7. **Serve:**
   1. Enjoy the muffins warm or at room temperature. They're great with a bit of butter or jam.

Tips:

- **Buttermilk Substitute:** If you don't have buttermilk, you can make your own by adding 1 tablespoon of lemon juice or white vinegar to 1 cup of milk. Let it sit for about 5 minutes before using.
- **Mix-Ins:** Feel free to add other mix-ins like chopped nuts, seeds, or dried fruit based on your preferences.
- **Storage:** Store leftover muffins in an airtight container at room temperature for up to 3 days, or freeze for up to 3 months.

These Irish Brown Bread Muffins offer a wholesome and satisfying twist on classic muffins, bringing a touch of Irish tradition to your baking. Enjoy making and savoring these delicious treats!

Mint Chocolate Chip Cheesecake

Ingredients:

For the Crust:

- 1 1/2 cups (150 g) chocolate cookie crumbs (e.g., Oreo cookies)
- 1/4 cup (50 g) granulated sugar

- 6 tablespoons (85 g) unsalted butter, melted

For the Cheesecake Filling:

- 4 (8 oz each) packages cream cheese, softened (32 oz total)
- 1 cup (200 g) granulated sugar
- 1 cup (240 ml) sour cream
- 1/2 cup (120 ml) heavy cream
- 4 large eggs
- 1 teaspoon vanilla extract
- 1 teaspoon peppermint extract
- Green food coloring (optional)
- 1 cup (175 g) mini chocolate chips (or chopped chocolate)

For the Whipped Cream Topping (optional):

- 1 cup (240 ml) heavy cream
- 2 tablespoons (15 g) powdered sugar
- 1/2 teaspoon vanilla extract

For Garnish (optional):

- Additional mini chocolate chips
- Fresh mint leaves

Instructions:

1. **Prepare the Crust:**
    1. Preheat your oven to 325°F (160°C).
    2. In a medium bowl, combine the chocolate cookie crumbs, granulated sugar, and melted butter. Mix until the crumbs are evenly coated and the mixture resembles wet sand.
    3. Press the mixture into the bottom of a 9-inch (23 cm) springform pan to form an even crust. Use the back of a spoon to press it down firmly.
    4. Bake the crust in the preheated oven for 8-10 minutes. Remove from the oven and let it cool while you prepare the filling.
2. **Prepare the Cheesecake Filling:**
    1. In a large mixing bowl, beat the softened cream cheese until smooth and creamy using an electric mixer.
    2. Add the granulated sugar and continue to beat until well combined and smooth.
    3. Mix in the sour cream and heavy cream until fully incorporated.
    4. Beat in the eggs one at a time, making sure each egg is fully mixed in before adding the next.
    5. Stir in the vanilla extract and peppermint extract. If you want a green hue, add a few drops of green food coloring and mix until evenly colored.
    6. Gently fold in the mini chocolate chips or chopped chocolate.

3. **Bake the Cheesecake:**
    1. Pour the cheesecake filling over the cooled crust in the springform pan.
    2. Smooth the top with a spatula.
    3. Bake in the preheated oven for 60-70 minutes, or until the center is set and only slightly jiggles when you shake the pan.
    4. Turn off the oven and crack the oven door slightly. Let the cheesecake cool in the oven for 1 hour to prevent cracking.
    5. Remove the cheesecake from the oven and refrigerate for at least 4 hours or overnight to fully set.
4. **Prepare the Whipped Cream Topping (optional):**
    1. In a mixing bowl, beat the heavy cream with the powdered sugar and vanilla extract until stiff peaks form.
    2. Spread or pipe the whipped cream over the top of the chilled cheesecake.
5. **Garnish and Serve:**
    1. Garnish with additional mini chocolate chips and fresh mint leaves if desired.
    2. Slice and serve chilled.

Tips:

- **Crust:** For an extra crunchy crust, you can bake it for a few extra minutes, but be careful not to burn it.
- **Cheesecake Cracking:** To minimize cracking, ensure your ingredients are at room temperature and avoid over-mixing the batter.
- **Chilling:** The cheesecake must be well-chilled to slice cleanly and have the right texture.

This Mint Chocolate Chip Cheesecake is a delightful blend of creamy, minty, and chocolaty flavors, perfect for any special occasion or just as a treat for yourself. Enjoy!

Lucky Charms Marshmallow Treats

Ingredients:

- 6 cups (180 g) Lucky Charms cereal
- 5 cups (about 200 g) mini marshmallows (or 10 oz of regular marshmallows)
- 1/4 cup (60 g) unsalted butter
- 1/2 teaspoon vanilla extract (optional)
- A pinch of salt (optional)

Instructions:

1. **Prepare the Pan:**
   1. Grease a 9x13-inch baking pan with butter or cooking spray, or line it with parchment paper for easy removal.
2. **Melt the Butter and Marshmallows:**
   1. In a large saucepan, melt the butter over medium heat.
   2. Add the mini marshmallows to the melted butter. Stir continuously until the marshmallows are completely melted and smooth. If using regular marshmallows, this might take a little longer, and you may need to stir more frequently.
   3. Once melted, you can stir in the vanilla extract and a pinch of salt if desired.
3. **Combine with Cereal:**
   1. Remove the saucepan from heat.
   2. Add the Lucky Charms cereal to the marshmallow mixture. Stir gently until the cereal is evenly coated with the marshmallow mixture.
4. **Press into Pan:**
   1. Transfer the mixture into the prepared baking pan.
   2. Use a spatula or a piece of wax paper to press the mixture evenly and firmly into the pan. Be gentle to avoid crushing the cereal too much.
5. **Cool and Slice:**
   1. Allow the treats to cool completely at room temperature before slicing. This usually takes about 30 minutes to 1 hour.
   2. Once set, cut into squares or rectangles.
6. **Serve:**
   1. Enjoy the treats as a fun and festive snack. They are best enjoyed within a few days of making.

Tips:

- **Butter:** Make sure the butter is fully melted before adding the marshmallows to prevent lumps.
- **Mixing:** Gently fold the cereal into the marshmallow mixture to keep the cereal pieces from breaking too much.
- **Storage:** Store the treats in an airtight container at room temperature for up to 5 days. They can also be stored in the refrigerator to keep them a bit firmer.

These Lucky Charms Marshmallow Treats are not only delicious but also visually appealing with their colorful marshmallows and crisp texture. They're sure to be a hit with kids and adults alike! Enjoy!

St. Patrick's Day Mini Bundt Cakes

Ingredients:

For the Mini Bundt Cakes:

- 1 1/2 cups (190 g) all-purpose flour
- 1 teaspoon baking powder
- 1/2 teaspoon baking soda
- 1/4 teaspoon salt
- 1/2 cup (115 g) unsalted butter, softened

- 1 cup (200 g) granulated sugar
- 2 large eggs
- 1 teaspoon vanilla extract
- 1/2 cup (120 ml) sour cream
- 1/4 cup (60 ml) milk (or Irish cream liqueur for added flavor)
- Green food coloring (gel or liquid, optional)

For the Glaze:

- 1 cup (120 g) powdered sugar
- 2-3 tablespoons milk or cream
- 1/4 teaspoon vanilla extract
- Green and gold sprinkles (optional)

Instructions:

1. **Prepare the Oven and Pan:**
    1. Preheat your oven to 350°F (175°C).
    2. Grease and flour mini bundt cake pans or spray them with a non-stick baking spray. If using a silicone pan, there's no need to grease.
2. **Prepare the Cake Batter:**
    1. In a medium bowl, whisk together the all-purpose flour, baking powder, baking soda, and salt.
    2. In a large mixing bowl, beat the softened butter and granulated sugar until light and fluffy.
    3. Add the eggs one at a time, beating well after each addition.
    4. Mix in the vanilla extract.
    5. Gradually add the flour mixture, alternating with the sour cream and milk (or Irish cream liqueur), beginning and ending with the flour mixture. Mix until just combined.
    6. If desired, add a few drops of green food coloring to the batter and mix until the color is evenly distributed.
3. **Fill the Bundt Pans:**
    1. Divide the batter evenly among the mini bundt pans, filling each about 2/3 full.
    2. Gently tap the pans on the counter to remove any air bubbles and level the batter.
4. **Bake:**
    1. Bake in the preheated oven for 15-20 minutes, or until a toothpick inserted into the center comes out clean.
    2. Let the cakes cool in the pans for about 5 minutes, then transfer them to a wire rack to cool completely.
5. **Prepare the Glaze:**
    1. In a small bowl, whisk together the powdered sugar, milk (or cream), and vanilla extract until smooth. Adjust the consistency by adding more powdered sugar or milk if necessary.

2. Drizzle the glaze over the cooled mini bundt cakes.
6. **Decorate:**
   1. If desired, sprinkle green and gold sprinkles on top of the glazed cakes for a festive touch.
7. **Serve:**
   1. Enjoy the mini bundt cakes as a delightful St. Patrick's Day treat.

Tips:

- **Flavors:** Feel free to experiment with different flavors in the cake batter, such as adding a bit of lemon zest or almond extract.
- **Consistency:** If you prefer a thicker glaze, add less milk; for a thinner glaze, add more.
- **Storage:** Store the mini bundt cakes in an airtight container at room temperature for up to 4 days. They can also be frozen for up to 3 months.

These St. Patrick's Day Mini Bundt Cakes are not only visually appealing with their festive decorations but also delicious and perfect for sharing with friends and family. Enjoy baking and celebrating!

Green Sugar Cookie Bars

Ingredients:

For the Bars:

- 2 1/4 cups (280 g) all-purpose flour
- 1/2 teaspoon baking soda
- 1/2 teaspoon baking powder
- 1/4 teaspoon salt
- 1 cup (225 g) unsalted butter, softened

- 1 1/4 cups (250 g) granulated sugar
- 1 large egg
- 1 teaspoon vanilla extract
- 1/2 teaspoon almond extract (optional)
- Green food coloring (gel or liquid)

For the Frosting:

- 1/2 cup (115 g) unsalted butter, softened
- 2 cups (240 g) powdered sugar
- 2 tablespoons milk or heavy cream (adjust as needed)
- 1/2 teaspoon vanilla extract
- Green food coloring (gel or liquid)
- Sprinkles or edible glitter (optional, for decoration)

Instructions:

1. **Prepare the Oven and Pan:**
    1. Preheat your oven to 350°F (175°C).
    2. Line a 9x13-inch baking pan with parchment paper, leaving an overhang for easy removal. Alternatively, you can lightly grease the pan.
2. **Make the Cookie Dough:**
    1. In a medium bowl, whisk together the flour, baking soda, baking powder, and salt.
    2. In a large bowl, beat the softened butter and granulated sugar together until light and fluffy.
    3. Add the egg, vanilla extract, and almond extract (if using), and mix until combined.
    4. Gradually add the dry ingredients to the wet ingredients, mixing until just combined.
    5. Add a few drops of green food coloring to the dough until you reach the desired shade of green. Mix until the color is evenly distributed.
3. **Bake the Bars:**
    1. Spread the cookie dough evenly into the prepared baking pan, smoothing it out with a spatula.
    2. Bake in the preheated oven for 20-25 minutes, or until the edges are lightly golden and the center is set.
    3. Let the bars cool completely in the pan on a wire rack before frosting.
4. **Prepare the Frosting:**
    1. In a medium bowl, beat the softened butter until creamy.
    2. Gradually add the powdered sugar, one cup at a time, beating well after each addition.
    3. Mix in the milk or heavy cream, vanilla extract, and green food coloring until smooth and spreadable. Adjust the consistency by adding more powdered sugar or milk if necessary.
5. **Frost and Decorate:**

1. Once the cookie bars are completely cooled, spread the green frosting evenly over the top.
   2. Sprinkle with additional decorations, such as sprinkles or edible glitter, if desired.
6. **Serve:**
   1. Lift the bars out of the pan using the parchment paper overhang, and cut into squares or rectangles.
   2. Serve and enjoy!

Tips:

- **Consistency:** If the frosting is too thick, add a little more milk or cream. If it's too thin, add more powdered sugar.
- **Coloring:** Use gel food coloring for a more vibrant color without affecting the consistency of the dough or frosting.
- **Storage:** Store the bars in an airtight container at room temperature for up to 4 days. They can also be refrigerated for up to a week.

These Green Sugar Cookie Bars are a fun and festive way to celebrate any occasion with a burst of color and delicious flavor. Enjoy baking and sharing these sweet treats!

Irish Cream Fudge

Ingredients:

- 2 cups (400 g) granulated sugar
- 1/2 cup (115 g) unsalted butter
- 1/2 cup (120 ml) heavy cream
- 1/2 cup (120 ml) Irish cream liqueur
- 1 cup (170 g) white chocolate chips or chopped white chocolate
- 1 teaspoon vanilla extract
- A pinch of salt

Instructions:

1. **Prepare the Pan:**
    1. Line an 8x8-inch baking pan with parchment paper, leaving an overhang for easy removal. Alternatively, you can lightly grease the pan.
2. **Cook the Fudge Base:**
    1. In a medium saucepan, combine the granulated sugar, unsalted butter, and heavy cream.
    2. Cook over medium heat, stirring constantly until the mixture comes to a boil.
    3. Once boiling, continue to cook while stirring for about 4-5 minutes, or until the mixture reaches the soft-ball stage (approximately 238°F or 114°C on a candy thermometer).
3. **Add Irish Cream Liqueur:**
    1. Remove the saucepan from heat.
    2. Stir in the Irish cream liqueur. Be cautious as the mixture may bubble up slightly.
4. **Incorporate White Chocolate:**
    1. Add the white chocolate chips or chopped white chocolate to the mixture.
    2. Stir until the chocolate is completely melted and the mixture is smooth.
    3. Stir in the vanilla extract and a pinch of salt.
5. **Pour and Set:**
    1. Pour the fudge mixture into the prepared baking pan.
    2. Smooth the top with a spatula to ensure it's even.
6. **Cool and Cut:**
    1. Allow the fudge to cool at room temperature until it is set, which usually takes about 2-3 hours.
    2. Once set, lift the fudge out of the pan using the parchment paper overhang and cut into squares or rectangles.
7. **Serve:**
    1. Enjoy the fudge as a rich, flavorful treat. Store in an airtight container at room temperature for up to 1 week, or refrigerate for longer storage.

Tips:

- **Texture:** If you prefer a softer fudge, you can reduce the cooking time slightly. For a firmer texture, cook until the mixture reaches the soft-ball stage.
- **Flavor Variations:** You can add a sprinkle of sea salt on top of the fudge before it sets for an extra touch of flavor.
- **Serving:** For a more festive presentation, you can garnish the fudge with crushed nuts or drizzle with additional melted white chocolate.

Irish Cream Fudge is a creamy, indulgent treat with a hint of Irish flair that's perfect for sharing with friends and family or enjoying on your own. Enjoy making and savoring this delicious dessert!

Shamrock Pie

Ingredients:

For the Crust:

- 1 1/2 cups (150 g) graham cracker crumbs
- 1/4 cup (50 g) granulated sugar
- 6 tablespoons (85 g) unsalted butter, melted

For the Filling:

- 1 cup (240 ml) heavy cream
- 1 cup (240 ml) whole milk
- 3/4 cup (150 g) granulated sugar
- 1/4 cup (30 g) cornstarch
- 1/4 teaspoon salt
- 4 large egg yolks
- 2 tablespoons unsalted butter
- 1 teaspoon vanilla extract
- 1 teaspoon peppermint extract (or mint extract for a different flavor)
- Green food coloring (gel or liquid, as needed)

For the Whipped Cream Topping:

- 1 cup (240 ml) heavy cream
- 2 tablespoons (15 g) powdered sugar
- 1/2 teaspoon vanilla extract

For Garnish (optional):

- Green sprinkles or edible glitter
- Fresh mint leaves

Instructions:

1. **Prepare the Crust:**
    1. Preheat your oven to 350°F (175°C).
    2. In a medium bowl, mix the graham cracker crumbs, granulated sugar, and melted butter until the mixture resembles wet sand.
    3. Press the mixture into the bottom and up the sides of a 9-inch (23 cm) pie dish to form an even crust.
    4. Bake the crust for 8-10 minutes, or until lightly golden. Remove from the oven and let it cool completely.
2. **Make the Filling:**
    1. In a medium saucepan, whisk together the heavy cream, whole milk, granulated sugar, cornstarch, and salt.
    2. Cook over medium heat, stirring constantly until the mixture begins to thicken and comes to a gentle boil. This should take about 5-7 minutes.
    3. In a separate bowl, lightly whisk the egg yolks.
    4. Gradually whisk a small amount of the hot milk mixture into the egg yolks to temper them, then whisk the egg yolk mixture back into the saucepan.
    5. Continue to cook the mixture for another 2-3 minutes, or until it's thick and creamy.
    6. Remove from heat and stir in the butter, vanilla extract, peppermint extract, and green food coloring until the desired shade of green is achieved.

7. Pour the filling into the cooled graham cracker crust and smooth the top with a spatula.

3. **Cool and Set:**
    1. Allow the pie to cool to room temperature.
    2. Refrigerate for at least 4 hours, or until the filling is fully set.
4. **Prepare the Whipped Cream Topping:**
    1. In a large bowl, beat the heavy cream, powdered sugar, and vanilla extract until stiff peaks form.
    2. Spread or pipe the whipped cream over the top of the set pie.
5. **Garnish and Serve:**
    1. Garnish with green sprinkles, edible glitter, or fresh mint leaves if desired.
    2. Slice and serve chilled.

Tips:

- **Consistency:** For a firmer filling, ensure the custard is cooked until it reaches a thick consistency. For a softer filling, you can slightly reduce the cooking time.
- **Color:** Use gel food coloring for a more vibrant and stable color.
- **Decorations:** You can use a star tip to pipe the whipped cream for a decorative effect.

Shamrock Pie is a visually stunning and delicious dessert that will impress your guests and add a festive touch to any celebration. Enjoy making and eating this delightful treat!

Green Velvet Cake Pops

Ingredients:

For the Cake:

- 1 1/2 cups (190 g) all-purpose flour
- 1 cup (200 g) granulated sugar
- 1/2 cup (115 g) unsalted butter, softened
- 1/2 cup (120 ml) buttermilk
- 2 large eggs

- 1 tablespoon green food coloring (gel or liquid)
- 1 tablespoon cocoa powder
- 1 teaspoon vanilla extract
- 1/2 teaspoon baking powder
- 1/2 teaspoon baking soda
- 1/4 teaspoon salt

For the Cream Cheese Frosting:

- 4 oz (115 g) cream cheese, softened
- 1/4 cup (60 g) unsalted butter, softened
- 1 1/2 cups (190 g) powdered sugar
- 1/2 teaspoon vanilla extract

For the Coating:

- 1 cup (175 g) candy melts or white chocolate, melted (green or other colors for coating)
- Sprinkles or edible glitter (optional, for decoration)

For the Cake Pop Sticks:

- Lollipop sticks or popsicle sticks

Instructions:

1. **Bake the Cake:**
    1. Preheat your oven to 350°F (175°C). Grease and flour an 8-inch (20 cm) round cake pan, or line it with parchment paper.
    2. In a medium bowl, whisk together the flour, cocoa powder, baking powder, baking soda, and salt.
    3. In a large bowl, cream the softened butter and granulated sugar until light and fluffy.
    4. Add the eggs one at a time, beating well after each addition.
    5. Mix in the vanilla extract and green food coloring until well combined.
    6. Gradually add the dry ingredients to the butter mixture, alternating with the buttermilk, beginning and ending with the dry ingredients. Mix until just combined.
    7. Pour the batter into the prepared cake pan and smooth the top.
    8. Bake for 25-30 minutes, or until a toothpick inserted into the center comes out clean.
    9. Let the cake cool completely in the pan before removing and crumbling into small pieces.
2. **Prepare the Cream Cheese Frosting:**
    1. In a medium bowl, beat together the softened cream cheese and butter until creamy.
    2. Gradually add the powdered sugar, mixing until smooth and fluffy.
    3. Mix in the vanilla extract.

3. **Make the Cake Pops:**
    1. In a large bowl, combine the crumbled cake with the cream cheese frosting. Mix until the mixture is well combined and holds together when pressed.
    2. Roll the mixture into 1-inch (2.5 cm) balls and place them on a baking sheet lined with parchment paper.
    3. Chill the cake balls in the refrigerator for at least 30 minutes, or until firm.
4. **Dip the Cake Pops:**
    1. Melt the candy melts or white chocolate according to the package instructions.
    2. Dip the end of a lollipop stick into the melted candy and then insert it into a cake ball. This helps to secure the stick in place.
    3. Dip each cake pop into the melted candy, making sure it is fully coated.
    4. Tap off any excess coating and place the cake pops back on the parchment paper to set.
    5. Optionally, add sprinkles or edible glitter before the coating sets.
5. **Serve:**
    1. Once the coating has hardened, the cake pops are ready to enjoy.
    2. Store any leftovers in an airtight container at room temperature for up to 5 days or refrigerate for longer storage.

Tips:

- **Consistency:** Make sure the cake crumbs and frosting are well combined for a smooth and easy-to-roll mixture.
- **Coating:** Use a block of chocolate or candy melts for the coating to ensure a smooth, even finish.
- **Decoration:** Feel free to get creative with decorations, such as using colored sprinkles or drizzling with additional melted chocolate.

These Green Velvet Cake Pops are a fun and festive treat that will add a touch of color and delight to any celebration. Enjoy making and sharing these tasty little bites!

Mint Oreo Cheesecake Bars

Ingredients:

For the Crust:

- 1 1/2 cups (150 g) crushed Mint Oreo cookies (about 15-18 cookies)
- 1/4 cup (50 g) granulated sugar
- 1/4 cup (60 g) unsalted butter, melted

For the Cheesecake Filling:

- 16 oz (450 g) cream cheese, softened
- 1 cup (200 g) granulated sugar
- 1 teaspoon vanilla extract
- 2 large eggs
- 1/2 cup (120 ml) sour cream
- 1/2 cup (120 ml) heavy cream
- 1/2 cup (120 g) chopped Mint Oreo cookies (about 8-10 cookies)

For the Topping:

- 1/2 cup (120 ml) heavy cream
- 1/2 cup (60 g) powdered sugar
- 1/4 teaspoon vanilla extract
- Crushed Mint Oreo cookies (optional, for garnish)

Instructions:

1. **Prepare the Oven and Pan:**
    1. Preheat your oven to 325°F (160°C).
    2. Line an 8x8-inch (20x20 cm) baking pan with parchment paper, leaving an overhang for easy removal. Alternatively, you can lightly grease the pan.
2. **Make the Crust:**
    1. In a medium bowl, mix the crushed Mint Oreo cookies with granulated sugar and melted butter until well combined.
    2. Press the mixture evenly into the bottom of the prepared baking pan to form the crust.
    3. Bake the crust for 8-10 minutes, or until it is set. Remove from the oven and let it cool slightly.
3. **Prepare the Cheesecake Filling:**
    1. In a large bowl, beat the softened cream cheese with granulated sugar until smooth and creamy.
    2. Mix in the vanilla extract.
    3. Add the eggs one at a time, beating well after each addition.
    4. Mix in the sour cream and heavy cream until the mixture is smooth.
    5. Fold in the chopped Mint Oreo cookies.
4. **Assemble and Bake:**
    1. Pour the cheesecake filling over the pre-baked crust and spread it evenly.
    2. Bake in the preheated oven for 35-40 minutes, or until the cheesecake is set and the edges are slightly golden. The center should still be slightly jiggly.
    3. Turn off the oven and let the cheesecake bars cool in the oven with the door slightly ajar for about 1 hour.
    4. Remove from the oven and refrigerate for at least 4 hours, or overnight, to allow the cheesecake to fully set.
5. **Prepare the Topping:**

1. In a medium bowl, whip the heavy cream, powdered sugar, and vanilla extract until stiff peaks form.
   2. Spread or pipe the whipped cream over the cooled cheesecake bars.
   3. Garnish with additional crushed Mint Oreo cookies, if desired.
6. **Serve:**
   1. Lift the cheesecake bars out of the pan using the parchment paper overhang and cut into squares or rectangles.
   2. Serve chilled and enjoy!

Tips:

- **Texture:** For a smoother cheesecake filling, make sure the cream cheese is fully softened before mixing.
- **Flavor:** Adjust the amount of chopped Mint Oreo cookies based on your preference for mint flavor and texture.
- **Storage:** Store the cheesecake bars in an airtight container in the refrigerator for up to 1 week. They can also be frozen for up to 3 months. If freezing, omit the whipped cream topping until ready to serve.

These Mint Oreo Cheesecake Bars are a perfect blend of creamy, minty, and crunchy, making them a delightful treat for any occasion. Enjoy baking and indulging in this delicious dessert!

Leprechaun Cupcake Jars

Ingredients:

For the Cupcakes:

- 1 1/2 cups (190 g) all-purpose flour
- 1 cup (200 g) granulated sugar
- 1/2 cup (115 g) unsalted butter, softened
- 1/2 cup (120 ml) milk

- 2 large eggs
- 1 1/2 teaspoons baking powder
- 1/2 teaspoon baking soda
- 1/4 teaspoon salt
- 1 teaspoon vanilla extract
- Green food coloring (gel or liquid)

For the Frosting:

- 1 cup (230 g) unsalted butter, softened
- 4 cups (480 g) powdered sugar
- 2-3 tablespoons heavy cream or milk
- 1 teaspoon vanilla extract
- Green food coloring (gel or liquid)
- Rainbow sprinkles or edible glitter (for decoration)

For Garnish:

- Mini marshmallows
- Gold or green edible glitter (optional)

For the Jars:

- 12 oz (350 ml) mason jars or similar-sized glass jars

Instructions:

1. **Prepare the Cupcakes:**
    1. Preheat your oven to 350°F (175°C). Line a cupcake pan with paper liners.
    2. In a medium bowl, whisk together the flour, baking powder, baking soda, and salt.
    3. In a large bowl, cream the softened butter and granulated sugar until light and fluffy.
    4. Add the eggs one at a time, beating well after each addition.
    5. Mix in the vanilla extract.
    6. Gradually add the dry ingredients to the butter mixture, alternating with the milk, beginning and ending with the dry ingredients. Mix until just combined.
    7. Add a few drops of green food coloring to the batter and mix until you reach the desired shade of green.
    8. Divide the batter evenly among the cupcake liners, filling each about 2/3 full.
    9. Bake for 15-18 minutes, or until a toothpick inserted into the center comes out clean.
    10. Allow the cupcakes to cool completely on a wire rack.
2. **Prepare the Frosting:**
    1. In a large bowl, beat the softened butter until creamy.
    2. Gradually add the powdered sugar, one cup at a time, mixing well after each addition.

3. Add 2 tablespoons of heavy cream or milk and the vanilla extract, and beat until smooth and fluffy. Add more milk if needed to reach the desired consistency.
4. Add green food coloring to the frosting and mix until the color is evenly distributed.

3. **Assemble the Cupcake Jars:**
    1. Once the cupcakes are completely cooled, crumble them into small pieces.
    2. In each mason jar, start by adding a layer of cupcake crumbles.
    3. Add a layer of green frosting on top of the cupcake crumbles.
    4. Repeat the layers until the jar is filled, finishing with a layer of frosting.
4. **Decorate:**
    1. Pipe additional frosting on top of the jars if desired.
    2. Garnish with rainbow sprinkles, mini marshmallows, and edible glitter to create a festive look.
5. **Serve:**
    1. Seal the jars with their lids and keep them refrigerated until ready to serve.
    2. Enjoy these fun and festive Leprechaun Cupcake Jars!

Tips:

- **Texture:** If you want a smoother frosting, ensure the butter is fully softened and beat the frosting until it's light and fluffy.
- **Coloring:** Use gel food coloring for a more vibrant color without affecting the consistency of the frosting.
- **Storage:** The assembled cupcake jars can be kept in the refrigerator for up to 3 days. They are best enjoyed within this time frame for freshness.

These Leprechaun Cupcake Jars are not only adorable but also delicious, making them a perfect treat for celebrating any occasion with a touch of whimsy. Enjoy making and sharing these delightful dessert jars!

www.ingramcontent.com/pod-product-compliance
Lightning Source LLC
LaVergne TN
LVHW061938070526
838199LV00060B/3873